The Hardships of the English Laws in Relation to Wives

Susan Paterson Glover here presents, in modern type, a critical edition of the first printed work by an English woman writer, Sarah Chapone, on the inequity of the common law regime for married women. Glover's extended, original introduction provides an account of Chapone's life; a discussion of the influence of Mary Astell's work on Chapone's thought and work; and a review of the legal status of women in England's eighteenth century, with particular attention to marriage and the doctrine of coverture and the relations of women, law, and property. It concludes by acknowledging the importance of this text to any consideration of the evolution of a discourse of "rights" for women in the Anglo–American legal tradition, and its contribution to a movement for property rights and women's equality whose genesis is generally located in the legislative changes of the nineteenth century. The edition contains valuable appendices including, among other writings, excerpts from Chapone's correspondence with Samuel Richardson; excerpts of responses to Chapone's work from the *Weekly Miscellany*; and excerpts from contemporary legal literature. Also included is an annotated text of Chapone's pamphlet on the Muilman controversy, *Remarks on Mrs. Muilman's Letter to the Right Honourable The Earl of Chesterfield* (London, 1750).

Susan Paterson Glover is Associate Professor of English at Laurentian University, Canada.

The Early Modern Englishwoman, 1500–1750

Edited by Betty S. Travitsky and Anne Lake Prescott

Designed to complement *The Early Modern Englishwoman: A Facsimile Library of Essential Works, Contemporary Editions* presents both modernized and old-spelling editions of texts not only by women but also for and about women. Contents of a volume can range from a single text to an anthology depending on the subject and the audience. Introductions to the editions are written with the general reader as well as the specialist in mind. They are designed to provide an introduction not only to the edited text itself but also to the larger historical discourses expressed through the text.

The Rival Widows, or Fair Libertine (1735)
Edited by Tiffany Potter

Elizabeth Tyrwhit's Morning and Evening Prayers
Edited by Susan M. Felch

Women, Madness and Sin in Early Modern England
The Autobiographical Writings of Dionys Fitzherbert
Edited by Katharine Hodgkin

The Correspondence (c. 1626–1659) of Dorothy Percy Sidney, Countess of Leicester
By Michael G. Brennan, Noel J. Kinnamon, edited by Margaret P. Hannay

The Experience of Domestic Service for Women in Early Modern London
Edited by Paula Humfrey

Two Early Modern Marriage Sermons
Henry Smith's A Preparative to Marriage (1591) and William Whately's A Bride-Bush (1623)
Edited by Robert Matz

The Collected Works of Jane Cavendish
Edited by Alexandra G. Bennett

The Hardships of the English Laws in Relation to Wives by Sarah Chapone
Edited by Susan Paterson Glover

The Hardships of the English Laws in Relation to Wives by Sarah Chapone

Edited by
Susan Paterson Glover

Routledge
Taylor & Francis Group

LONDON AND NEW YORK

First published 2018
by Routledge

2 Park Square, Milton Park, Abingdon, Oxfordshire OX14 4RN
52 Vanderbilt Avenue, New York, NY 10017

Routledge is an imprint of the Taylor & Francis Group, an informa business

First issued in paperback 2020

British Library Cataloguing-in-Publication Data
A catalogue record for this book is available from the British Library

Library of Congress Cataloging-in-Publication Data
Names: Chapone, Sarah Kirkham, 1699–1764. author. |
Glover, Susan, 1950– editor.
Title: The hardships of the English laws in relation to wives /
by Sarah Chapone ; edited by Susan Paterson Glover.
Description: New York : Routledge, 2017. |
Series: The early modern englishwoman, 1500–1750 : contemporary editions |
"Designed to complement The Early Modern Englishwoman :
A Facsimile Library of Essential Works", Contemporary Editions presents
both modernized and old-spelling editions of texts." |
Includes bibliographical references and index.
Identifiers: LCCN 2016031041 | ISBN 9781409450771 (alk. paper)
Subjects: LCSH: Husband and wife—England—Early works to 1800. |
Women—Legal status, laws, etc.—England—Early works to 1800.
Classification: LCC KD758 .C43 1735 | DDC 342.4208/78—dc23
LC record available at https://lccn.loc.gov/2016031041

ISBN: 978-1-4094-5077-1 (hbk)
ISBN: 978-0-367-59300-1 (pbk)

Typeset in Times New Roman
by Florence Production Ltd, Stoodleigh, Devon, UK

For Findlay Paterson Bergstra (1983–2006),
and the house in Oxford

Contents

Acknowledgements

It is a commonplace to begin these expressions of acknowledgement with a recognition of the collaborative nature of scholarship, and over the years this work has been in preparation I have amassed many debts. My introduction to eighteenth-century law and literature was supported by the serendipitous resources of the special collections and the scholars of the University of Toronto: John Baird, John Beattie, Pat Brückmann, Douglas Chambers, Brian Corman, Tom Keymer, Carol Percy, and Jim Phillips, together with the guidance of then law librarian Balfour Halévy, Osgoode Hall Law School Library, York University, and his introduction to the world of the early books of the common law.

The research for this work was made possible by the kind assistance of librarians at the University of Toronto, in particular those at the Robarts and Thomas Fisher Rare Book Libraries; the Bodleian Library, Oxford University; the Methodist Archives, Manchester University Library; the Newport Public Library in Wales; and the Gloucestershire Archives, with special thanks to Ashley Thomson and the generous staff of the J. N. Desmarais Library, Laurentian University. I also acknowledge two Laurentian University Research Fund awards that supported this research.

I am grateful to the Thomas Fisher Rare Book Library, University of Toronto, for permission to use its copy of *The Hardships of the English Laws in Relation to Wives* as the copy text, and to the late Richard Landon for its acquisition; my appreciation as well to Jocelyn Harris for sharing a paper on Samuel Richardson, to Lynne Greenberg for her introduction to *Legal Treatises*, to Marc Hight for information about Bishop Berkeley, and to Richard Heitzenrater for his work on John Wesley's diaries. To the Women's Legal and Education Action Fund of Canada (LEAF), whose work I was privileged to be part of during the preparation of this edition, may Chapone's voice remind us all of the women who went before.

To Patti Brace, Shannon Hengen, Chantel Lavoie, Jenny McKenny, Marilyn Orr, Carol Stos, Elizabeth Urso, Maria Zytaruk and to M&P and the comforts of Manning Street, my thanks for friendship, counsel, and hospitality. I am very grateful to Series Editors Betty S. Travitsky and Anne Lake Prescott, and to Erika Gaffney and the anonymous readers at Ashgate for their guidance on earlier drafts of the manuscript, and to Nicole Eno, Jennifer Abbott, Michelle Salyga, and Timothy Swenarton at Routledge/Taylor and Francis for seeing it through. To Jess Bithrey and Florence Production for the professional and detailed attention turning manuscript into book, my deepest appreciation; any errors that remain are my own. And to my family, *slàinte*.

A Note on the Texts

The Hardships of the English Laws in Relation to Wives was published anonymously in 1735; in London in an octavo edition printed by William Bowyer for James Roberts, and in Dublin, in a duodecimo edition printed by and for George Faulkner. This edition takes as its copy text the London edition held at the Thomas Fisher Rare Book Library, University of Toronto, Toronto, Ontario, Canada. The long "s" has been modernized, as has the use of running marginal quotation marks; otherwise the text has been preserved. The copy text for *Remarks on Mrs. Muilman's Letter to the Right Honourable the Earl of Chesterfield. In a Letter to Mrs. Muilman. By a Lady* (London and Bath, 1750), is held in the Sterling Memorial Library, Yale University, available on microfilm in "History of Women," New Haven, CT: Research Publications, 1975; the work is also available in Gale Cengage's *Eighteenth Century Collections Online*.

A Note on the Spelling of "Chapone"

Sarah Chapone's name appears in eighteenth-century archival sources with a variety of spellings: Capon, Capoon, Capone, Chapon, and Chapone. Her husband's name was John Capon, and all early documentation is clearly "Capon" in school, university, and parish records. One helpful guide is the survey of Gloucester parishes by Bishop Benson: in the first two surveys covering 1735–1738, the spelling is "Capon," but with the final survey dating from 1750, all the references are spelled "Chapone."[1] From the letters in the Ballard Manuscripts, Elizabeth Elstob, writing in the 1730s, uses "Chapon," and Chapone herself signs a letter to Mrs. Knightly as "Sarah Capon" in 1736, but her letters written in the 1740s have "Chapone." All references to the children's names that I have seen are spelled "Chapone," as is Hester Mulso's married name.

Note

1   Martin Benson, *Bishop Benson's Survey of the Diocese of Gloucester, 1735–50*, ed. John Findlay (The Bristol and Gloucestershire Archaeological Society, 2000).

THE
HARDSHIPS
OF THE
ENGLISH LAWS

In relation to

WIVES.

WITH AN

EXPLANATION of the ORIGINAL CURSE of
Subjection paſſed upon the WOMAN.

IN AN

Humble Addreſs to the LEGISLATURE.

---

*I could alſo ſpeak as ye do ; if your Soul were in my Souls Stead, I could
heap up Words againſt you, and ſhake mine Head at you.
But I would ſtrengthen you with my Mouth, and the moving of my Lips
ſhould aſſwage your Grief.
Tho' I ſpeak, my Grief is not aſſwaged; and tho' I forbear, what am I
eaſed? Job. xvi. 4, 5, 6.
For it was not an Enemy that reproached me, then I could have born it ;
neither was it he that hated me, that did magnifie himſelf againſt me,
then I would have hid my ſelf from him.
But it was thou, a Man, mine Equal, my Guide, and mine Acquaintance.
We took ſweet Counſel together, and walked into the Houſe of God in Company. Pſalm. lvi. 12, 13, 14.*

LONDON,
Printed by W. BOWYER, for J. ROBERTS, at the *Oxford
Arms in Warwick Lane.* MDCCXXXV.
(Price one Shilling.)

Introduction

A few years after the close of the American Revolution, the January 1788 issue of Philadelphia's monthly *Columbian Magazine* published the first of five parts of "A Tract on the Unreasonableness of the Laws of England in regard to Wives." The unidentified male author writes surprisingly sympathetically of the plight of wives, observing that while much of the inequality arises from biblical injunction, the realities of married life compound the disabilities in law; "when we refuse to bear our part of the curse, with what equity can we ask them to bear theirs?" After laying out a detailed and persuasive analysis of the rigors of the common law that keep married women at a severe disadvantage, he wonders rather daringly whether "all parts of a community have not a right to a degree of liberty and property, correspondent to the constitution under which they live." From there he concludes that it is pointless to argue that women would make poor use of such a right; "if the law of God and the rules of equity allow it them, they have a right to it."[1] There is no indication in the journal that the work had been published previously, and more importantly, that silent editing had altered the gender of the speaker, changing pronouns from "we" to "they." The tract was in fact published in England over fifty years earlier, and written by a woman.

Identified by Ruth Perry as the work of Sarah Chapone, *The Hardships of the English Laws* has received passing notice in a number of accounts of women's history, but it frequently remains unattributed.[2] Nevertheless, the importance of this text to any consideration of the evolution of a discourse of "rights" for women in the Anglo–American politico-legal tradition and its contribution to a movement for property rights and women's equality is immeasurable. What is particularly remarkable about Chapone's tract is that it is written for "everywoman." To a degree difficult to imagine today, the course of women's lives in England was shaped by the laws that governed inheritance, property, land transfers, and children; these laws reflected and reinforced the secondary status of women, particularly wives, determined in large measure by the consequence of the biblical Fall described in the book of Genesis that cursed and confined them to inferiority and submission.

Under England's common law a widow was entitled to her dower, usually one third of her deceased husband's estate in real property. By the early eighteenth century most married women, where significant property was involved, were under a legal settlement drawn up prior to marriage that specified a jointure to be paid in lieu of dower rights, should they be widowed. A bride was expected to bring a contribution of money (her portion) that became her husband's property, while he in turn arranged a jointure, often property in land for her lifetime should she outlive him. These arrangements were drawn up in a legal settlement (or a strict settlement, where the property was vested in trustees) and would include a quarterly allowance for personal expenses known as pin money. A single woman (*feme sole*) had a relative degree of legal freedom, could own property and other assets, and often had additional rights. Once married however (*feme covert*), a woman lost her legal existence and was unable to own property, enter into contracts, have her own money or income, or hold guardianship of her children. A husband acquired an absolute right to all his wife's personal property and all income from her real property (land) during her lifetime, apart from some items of clothing and jewels as defined by paraphernalia (see Appendix Two), and following her death for his lifetime if a child had been born during the marriage. Historians have investigated the gap between the prescription of law and the latitude of practice, and the difficulties in making assumptions about women's lives as they were lived from a reading of the law.[3] What makes Chapone's text so significant is its synthesis of the practices of law and observations drawn from reading and experience. It also provides a glimpse into one woman's struggle, beyond the urban centers of Great Britain and Europe where writers and philosophers gathered in salons and coffee houses to engage with the challenges of enlightenment thought, to reconcile for herself scriptural commands with an inchoate sense of disjunction between doctrine and reason.

Those few works that had addressed the matter of women under the law in England to that point—Sir Edward Coke's *The First Part of the Institutes of the Lawes of England*, known as *Coke on Littleton* (1628), T[homas] E[dgar]'s *The Lawes Resolutions of Womens Rights* (1632), *Baron and Feme* (1700), and *A Treatise of Feme Coverts* (1732)—covered the range of life events when women would come into relations with the law, but by far the greatest emphasis fell on the descent and transfer of property and women's primary role as "venters" (the legal term highlighting a wife's role as a "womb") to pass property from one generation of men to the next. Chapone's work, by contrast, addresses the daily experience of many married women's lives: the difficulties in keeping money and property that was theoretically at their own disposal; the vulnerability of those for whom there was little recourse if a husband proved abusive or withheld money; the inability to participate equally in the upbringing of children and the loss of custody should a husband die; above all the legal status of the *feme covert*, whose civil existence was suspended during coverture and Chapone's visceral and deeply felt awareness of the inequity and injustice of this reality.

* * *

Sarah Kirkham was born December 11, 1699 to Damaris (née Boyse, daughter of Robert and Damaris Boyse of Wellesbourne, Warwickshire) and Lionel Kirkham, son of the Rev. Henry Kirkham and Sarah Kirkham, in the village of Stanton, Gloucestershire, in the heart of the Cotswolds. Her father, like his father before him, was the rector of St. Michael and All Angels, and Sarah ("Sally" to her family) grew up in the rectory with her brothers Robert (1707) and Bernard (1719) and sisters Damaris (1701) and Mary Elizabeth (1709).[4] According to Robert Atkyns' *The Ancient and Present State of Glostershire* (1712) the parish included "60 *Houses* in this Parish, and about 300 *Inhabitants*, whereof 29 are *Freeholders*," and the rectory was worth £90 yearly; Vivian Green describes them as "the chief family in Stanton."[5] Susan Staves comments on women writers of the period that "a striking percentage of intellectually ambitious women publishing serious non-fiction had clergy fathers (or sometimes uncles or brothers) who contributed substantially to their educations." Sarah certainly fits this pattern, and surviving letters and journal entries of the Kirkham friends suggest a lively home where Sarah would have benefitted from the rectory library, the rectory conversations, and the educational preparation of two younger brothers for Oxford.[6]

Early Years

Sarah spent the entirety of her life in Gloucestershire and might have remained in complete obscurity were it not for accidents of fate that brought friendships with some of the best-known figures of the century. Following the failed Jacobite rebellion of 1715 Bernard Granville, the younger brother of George Granville, Lord Lansdowne, moved his family to the rural retreat of Buckland in the Cotswold hills. They settled at Buckland Manor, a short distance from the village of Stanton. His daughter Mary and Sarah struck up a fast friendship that lasted the remainder of Sarah's life, providing her a window into a world she would otherwise never have known. Mary had lived at Whitehall in London with an aunt and uncle, Lady Anne and Sir John Stanley, in training for a possible position at court, an experience very different from that of the siblings in the Stanton rectory of rural Gloucestershire. Mary's father initially disapproved of the friendship with Sarah, but soon came around; as Mary later recalled, Sarah had "an uncommon genius and intrepid spirit, which though really innocent, alarmed my father," but in time her "extraordinary understanding, lively imagination and humane disposition, which soon became conspicuous, at last reconciled my father to her."[7]

Bernard Granville may have had good reason for uneasiness with an independ-ent spirit; his brother Lord Lansdowne arranged a marriage in 1717 between Mary, aged seventeen, and his friend Alexander Pendarves, forty years her senior, following which they removed to his home in Cornwall. The marriage was not a happy one, and following Pendarves's unexpected death in 1725, the widowed Mary returned to London, but visited frequently with her mother and sister Anne who had moved to Gloucester following the death of Bernard Granville in 1723.[8] Over the years her friendship with Sarah inevitably altered as the disparity between their situations became more pronounced, and there are hints that Mary Pendarves later in life wished to preserve distinctions that would circumscribe the friendship between a rural clergyman's wife and a member of aristocratic circles who would count among her closest friends the Duchess of Portland, and later, the king and queen of England. At the same time Pendarves acknowledged and deeply admired Chapone's superior intellectual abilities. In April 1728 she wrote to her sister, "Enclosed I have sent you Sally's letter; pray take care of it, and send it me by the first opportunity, but I desire you will read this first, for you can never bear these trifles after *her solidity*."[9] A decade later, she continued to express her admiration for Chapone's abilities: "Sally would shine in an assembly composed of Tullys, Homers, and Miltons; at Gloucester she is like a diamond set in jet, their dulness makes her brightness brighter!"[10] Pendarves (later Delany), with no children of her own, worked assiduously over the years to assist members of Chapone's family, promoting the sons' interests with her various connections and ensuring the daughters had opportunities the Chapones could never have provided.

Marriage and Family

In April 1725, Sarah's brother Robert brought home to Stanton a fellow student from Oxford, John Wesley. During his university years Robert was involved with the Oxford Methodists, a group of students who gathered with Charles and later John Wesley for disciplined reading, devotions, and prayer. The Wesley brothers' visits to the Stanton rectory became frequent, and the young people in the Cotswold circle adopted names for themselves taken from ancient history and romance: Sarah was "Varanese" (and occasionally "Sappho"), her sister Elizabeth (Betty) was "Serena," Mary's sister Anne was "Selima," John Wesley was "Cyrus," and Charles was "Araspes." Mary Pendarves, introduced later to the group, was "Aspasia." Although Robert Kirkham and John Capon, the young vicar of neighboring Childswickham, were part of this group, there appears to be no evidence of their participation in the adoption of these personae.

In his authoritative study of Wesley, Henry Rack notes that a number of John Wesley's biographers have dated his religious awakening to this period (the conversion experience Wesley records occurred much later in London, in 1738), linking it to his discussions with the Kirkham/Chapone circle.[11] Sarah has also been credited with Wesley's formative reading of both Thomas à Kempis's *Imitation of Christ* and Jeremy Taylor's *Rules of Holy Living and Dying*. Although Sarah's engagement to John Capon had been announced around the time the Wesley brothers were introduced to the Stanton rectory, she and John Wesley developed a very close friendship, continuing after her marriage, and this relationship has proven a challenge for Wesley's biographers. As Wesley developed the theological understanding and devotional practices that would come to be known as Methodism, he and Sarah continued to correspond, and her letters suggest a continued attachment to both John and his brother Charles, though she clearly did not share the religious convictions that would lead him to his open-air preaching and appeals to the heart. Wesley's formidable mother Susanna Wesley more than once cautioned him about this friendship, reminding him that "What blooms beautifully sometimes bears bitter fruit."[12] Sarah and her friends lamented the public ridicule and abuse he endured but they remained unswayed by his ideas.

Elizabeth Elstob recounts a warm discussion between Sarah and Benjamin Seward (1705–1753), older brother to William Seward (1711–1740), a Methodist convert who died a year later, possibly as a result of an attack during rioting while he was preaching. (Another brother was the Rev. Thomas Seward (1708–1790), father of the writer Anna Seward.) Elstob worries about the consequences of his [Seward's] "miserable delusions" while Sarah emerges the victor.[13]

Wesley's biographers have speculated on the reasons why this attachment did not lead to marriage: whatever they may have been, a romantic relation did not prosper, and instead Sarah married John Capon on December 28, 1725. Little is known of his early life: his older brother David Capon was admitted a sizar to Trinity College, Cambridge, an exhibitioner from St. Paul's School, London in 1716, and graduated B.A. in 1720. John Capon was admitted to Trinity College from St. Paul's in 1719 but as a Fellow Commoner and graduated L.L.B. in 1725.[14] The marriage appears to have been a happy one and references in letters suggest that both Sarah and her husband (hereafter referred to as Sarah and John Chapone—see note on the spelling of "Chapone" p. xi) were involved in teaching, either keeping students in their home, or even running an independent boarding school. Her correspondence frequently alludes to the cares of teaching and raising a family; during the first ten years of their marriage, they had four surviving children: John (1727), Henry (1729), Sarah (1731), and Katherine (1732). The parish register also records a son baptized Lionel in 1728 who died the following year.

Gloucestershire Friendships

Despite the domestic demands in this period, Chapone turned some of her attention to the needs of a neighbor. In 1730 she wrote a letter of support for the Anglo-Saxon scholar Elizabeth Elstob, then living in penury and obscurity in nearby Evesham. Elstob had earlier enjoyed a remarkable period of scholarly life with her brother William in Oxford and London, and was widely recognized among her fellow antiquarians for her extraordinary achievements: she published *An English-Saxon Homily on the Birth-Day of St. Gregory* (1709) and *The Rudiments of Grammar for the English-Saxon Tongue* (1715), and had other ambitious projects in progress. All came to an end with the death of her brother in 1715, and Elstob was plunged into homelessness and poverty. She left London and seemed to disappear, but Chapone knew she was living at Evesham as "Frances Smith."[15] Chapone worked with a group of friends to find an alternative for her, and as part of the campaign wrote a letter to Queen Caroline requesting support. Pendarves arranged for the letter to be delivered to the queen, and reported to her sister in October 1730 that the Queen had read the letter and inquired not only about the person mentioned but about its author. "The Queen said she never in her Life read a better letter, that it had touched her heart, and ordered immediately an hundred pounds for Mrs. Elstob."[16] The efforts on behalf of Elstob bore fruit and eventually she was offered the position of tutor to the Duchess of Portland's children.

While living in London Elstob had known and admired the philosopher and writer Mary Astell and the surviving correspondence in the Ballard Manuscripts held at the Bodleian Library makes clear the influence of Astell's work and thought on Chapone and her circle. The letters include frequent references to copies of Astell's work to be loaned, exchanged, or returned. It is Astell's polemic on married life *Some Reflections Upon Marriage* (1700) and the preface added for the 1706 edition that seem particularly to have influenced Chapone.[17] It is possible that the 1730 editions of Astell's *Letters Concerning the Love of God, Some Reflections Upon Marriage,* and *The Christian Religion, as Profess'd by a Daughter of the Church of England* published shortly after her death may have renewed interest from the Cotswold group, but we know that Chapone was already reading Astell as a young woman.[18] Chapone admired not only her work on education and on women but also her religious views; she reported to George Ballard that Astell's letters to the philosopher and clergyman John Norris were "generally thought the most sublime part of her Works ."[19]

Chapone and the World of Print

It would appear that Chapone wrote her work on the law in the period immediately following the success of her letter on behalf of Elstob. The specific cases she cites in *The Hardships of the English Laws* were reported in the press through the early 1730s and John Wesley notes in his diary that he read the manuscript of her "Essay on Laws" in 1734. The work appeared anonymously in the spring of 1735, and apart from some attention from the *Gentleman's Magazine* and the *Weekly Miscellany*, and an admiring comment in a pamphlet defending the Quaker practice of allowing women to preach, it caused little controversy.[20] The publication of *Hardships* did not appear to open a new life of authorship for Chapone; in 1736 she wrote to a friend apologizing for falling behind in their correspondence and lamenting the lack of time for "Intellectual improvement." Her time was taken up with teaching and caring for six children, and both her husband and father suffered ill health.[21]

Chapone's friendship with Elstob led to another endeavor. On hearing that George Ballard, a local tailor and aspiring antiquarian, was teaching himself Anglo-Saxon she introduced him to Elizabeth Elstob. Ballard took up Elstob's proposal for a book about learned women in Great Britain, eventually published as *Memoirs of Several Ladies of Great Britain* in 1752. During the years of its compilation, Sarah wrote letters on his behalf, found and communicated with subscribers, commented on his writing, and helped finesse the dedication to her friend Mary, who in 1743 had married the Rev. Patrick Delany and settled in Ireland.[22] Chapone was able to make a substantive difference in Elstob's life and contributed enormously to the completion of Ballard's project (Ruth Perry notes he "acknowledged his debt to her in his will in which he left her his collection of books and papers concerning learned women") yet for both endeavors she could give only her time and her abilities.[23] In one of her letters to Ballard she apologizes that she has not yet been able to send the subscriber's fee, adverting to financial losses suffered by her husband, and neither she nor her husband appear on the subscription list.

She also appears to have at last found some time for her own writing. She writes to Ballard in 1749 that "Mr. Lyttleton's Book upon the Conversion of St. Paul" reflects some of her own ideas that she had written about earlier and sent to Dr. Delany. George Lyttelton's *Observations on the Conversion and Apostleship of St. Paul. In a letter to Gilbert West, Esq.* had reached a fourth edition in 1749. Delany had urged her to publish, but she is hesitant and would like to send her work to Lyttelton "through the hands of the Dean of Exeter" if he approves (the Dean was Lyttelton's younger brother Charles, a correspondent of Ballard's).[24] Chapone's early interest in theology is evident from her lengthy conversations with John Wesley in the Stanton rectory recorded in his diary. In the opening to *Hardships of the English Laws* she alludes to concerns about the rise of deism and the concomitant decline of Christian charity and mercy that might mitigate husbands' prerogatives. There are frequent and admiring references in her writing to Patrick Delany's *Revelation Examined* (1732). Mary Pendarves wrote to her sister in January 1733 that Sally was "in great Raptures with D.ʳ Delany's book on Revelation."[25]

However, it was not her theological reflections but rather her response to one of the "scandalous memoirists" that prompted her re-entry into the world of print. In 1748, the year the first volumes of Samuel Richardson's *Clarissa* appeared, two autobiographical works by women had caused a considerable stir. *An Apology for the Conduct of Mrs. Teresia Constantia Phillips* and the first volume of *Memoirs of Laetitia Pilkington* both contained frank descriptions of the misfortunes and abuse in early life that had led to "fallen" lives. The publications prompted widespread condemnation of the temerity of these women who not only had failed to exhibit sufficient contrition, but had the affrontery to publish candid accounts of their shameful lives. Constantia Phillips followed up the publication of her memoirs with a further defense of her conduct and a condemnation of the double standard that leaves women's lives irreparably damaged in *A Letter humbly address'd to the Right Honourable the Earl of Chesterfield* (1750). Chapone responded with *Remarks on Mrs. Muilman's Letter to the Right Honourable The Earl of Chesterfield*, published anonymously in London and Bath the same year.

There appears to be no clear evidence suggesting why Chapone might have chosen to respond to this work at this time, although there is an interesting parallel with Astell's response to the published accounts of another notorious woman, Hortense Mancini, Duchess of Mazarin. Married at fifteen to a wealthy but mentally unstable husband, she eventually became a mistress to Charles II, but died in 1699, deeply in debt, a model for Astell of the folly and futility of marriage motivated by worldly concerns. Astell opens her 1706 Preface to *Some Reflections upon Marriage* with an explanation that the work had been written "in the Country, where the Book that occasion'd them came but late to Hand." Scholars have suggested that the book alluded was related to this scandal.[26] Chapone's son Henry was living in Jamaica in the late 1740s as a victualing agent for the Boyd Company and may have heard tales of Phillips's residence there as the mistress of Henry Needham several years earlier. And it may be that Chapone took exception to Phillips's (well founded) condemnation of the law as a cover for what to Chapone was her sinful and unrepentant behavior.

In the event, Chapone's re-entry into the publishing world was to have far-reaching consequences for her and her entire family. In their biographical study of Samuel Richardson, T. C. Duncan Eaves and Ben D. Kimpel suggest that before their correspondence began,

> Richardson during the summer of 1750 read in manuscript and possibly printed her anonymous *Remarks on Mrs. Muilman's Letter to the Right Honourable The Earl of Chesterfield,* a polite but firm reproof of a fallen woman, whose apology had, in Mrs. Chapone's view, not shown humility and true penitence and who, in addition, had shown Deistic tendencies.[27]

Chapone first wrote to Richardson from Cheltenham October 12, 1750. She admits her authorship of the "papers" her son John had passed along for review (John, an attorney in London, had been introduced to Richardson through Delany's sister Anne Dewes), assuming he would recognize her handwriting, and worries that this loss of anonymity would preclude her submitting future work for his approval. She also requests that he keep her authorship a secret: "I could not bear to have my Name bandied about with Mrs. Muilman's. To be drawn out of my Obscurity in such Company, would give me great Disquiet."[28] Richardson replied with assurance of her continued anonymity and a flattering comment on the work's reception. In the wake of the "scandal memoirs" of Phillips and Pilkington, the "Memoirs of a Lady of Quality" inserted in the third volume of Tobias Smollett's *Peregrine Pickle* followed in 1751. The account of the extramarital adventures of Lady Vane, believed to have been written at least in part by her, titillated and shocked the novel's readers. Richardson proposed to Chapone that she write a response, similar to her reply to Muilman. After offering to send a copy (the novel was still in the press), he adds that Pilkington, Phillips, and Lady Vane are "a Set of Wretches" that would make "the Behn's, the Manley's, and the Heywood's look white" and that someone from the same sex should provide "the Antidote to these Womens Poison!"[29] Chapone replied February 1750/51 that she is "absolutely at a loss what to say;" despite her deference to his recommendation and judgment, she is clearly repelled by Vane's memoirs. Having reflected without success on how she might respond, she joins him in wishing that "some thing were done," and continues to ask his direction: clearly modesty is fighting with ambition and she needs more encouragement, but it is not forthcoming, and she apologizes that "Domestick perplexities" have taken up her time and thoughts.[30] In the event, it appears that no second response to scandalous women was undertaken.

Interest in Chapone's *Remarks* soon faded, but the connection and the correspondence with Richardson flourished. John Caroll's introduction to his edition of Richardson's correspondence notes that with Chapone "Richardson seems much more at his ease than in his epistles to other friends of Mrs. Delany," in part because Chapone was "not a bluestocking or a sophisticate of the West End."[31] Much of their epistolary conversation over the decade dwelled on family matters and visits of the daughters between the two families, but they also engaged in vigorous debate that included a sustained and deeply engaged discussion of the legal status of *Clarissa*'s eponymous heroine and possible right to an independent life.[32] As in his discussions with the young Hester Mulso, Richardson resists, at times testily, but Chapone gives no quarter, and although she compliments him on the sublimity of his writing, when she feels he has neglected what logic and reason would justify for women she is tenacious. Curiously, there is no mention in the surviving correspondence of her authorship of *Hardships*, yet many of her arguments are drawn from it and she occasionally quotes from it in her discussion (see Appendix Three). Despite their differences, Richardson clearly respected her, and Eaves and Kimpel report that by

> September 1753, two months before Richardson published the first four volumes of his novel [*Sir Charles Grandison*], Mrs. Chapone had read some of it, and Richardson promised to send her the third and fourth volumes, which no one else had, and did so.[33]

Although she had declined Richardson's request to respond to Lady Vane's memoir, Chapone may have been working on other projects. The Ballard correspondence provides evidence that Chapone was writing a theological work sent to Bishop George Berkeley for his review two years later. Letters to George Ballard written in 1752 indicate that she would like the Bishop's opinion on something, asking him to read her work and then convey it to the Bishop, who had recently moved to Oxford. A letter dated January 21, 1753 seems to indicate that she has just learned of the Bishop's death and is anxious to retrieve the papers she had sent to him. A few days later she writes that she has heard from Berkeley's son (George Monck Berkeley) that arrangements have been made to return her papers via her son.[34] The following October, in a letter to a friend Chapone adds,

> I have begun something, as an Inquiry concerning Truth; but have finished no Part of it. Great Interruptions of Health this Summer, and many troublesome Affairs, have prevented my making any Progress. When I can complete my Scheme, you shall see it; but when that will be, I cannot guess.[35]

Later Life and Loss

Chapone's correspondence with Richardson and the subsequent intercourse between the two families may have marked the high point of her later life. The remaining years would bring a series of losses, and she herself did not live to see the marriages of her daughters. There appear to have been continuing financial pressures, for Delany wrote to Anne Dewes in 1754 asking her to tell Sally that "I can't get enough for her uncle K[irkham]'s jewels," suggesting that Sarah had asked her to attempt to sell them.[36] Her younger son Henry died while in the West Indies and was buried in North Carolina in 1755, and four years later Chapone suffered the death of her husband. In addition to the emotional pain of widowhood, financial difficulties remained. Delany wrote to her sister in December noting that the younger John Chapone "has already paid the most considerable debts, tho' he cannot pay all at present."[37]

The connection with Richardson led to another significant consequence for the Chapone family. It was at his home in London that her son John met Hester Mulso in the fall of 1754, and they subsequently entered a lengthy engagement. Mulso, who would later become well known as a bluestocking and the author of Letters on the Improvement of the Mind (1773), had come to particular notice in the public response to Clarissa through an epistolary debate with Richardson over filial duty and obligation. The exchange between Mulso and Richardson was not published but was widely read in Richardson's circle and beyond, and Richardson believed his arguments had influenced the passage of Hardwicke's 1753 Marriage Act: references in Chapone's letters suggest that she had read, and supported, Mulso's views.[38] Despite the tribulations, in December of 1760 the long delayed marriage between John and Hester Mulso took place. After her wedding Hester Chapone wrote to Elizabeth Carter of her happiness, and of her new family connections. After noting her regret that she saw little of her sisters-in-law Sarah and Katherine she adds,

> I have a mother too, whom her son is as proud of as she is of him. But alas, I never saw her, and God knows whether I ever shall, for she grows infirm, and her constitution has been terribly shaken by the death of a son and a husband, both within a few years.[39]

Yet more blows lay in store. In July of 1761, both Samuel Richardson and Anne Dewes died, ending some of the most important of Chapone's remaining connections, and September brought the death of her son John. The widowed Hester Chapone spent much of the rest of her life with her own family, but it appears from occasional comments in Delany's correspondence that connections were maintained with her Chapone sisters-in-law.

Sarah Chapone died less than three years later, and was buried February 24, 1764 at Stanton, aged sixty four. She did not live to see the successful settling of her two daughters. Sarah (also known as Sally) married later that year the Rev. Dr. Daniel Sandford and they lived for a period of time with the Delanys in Ireland. Sandford eventually inherited his father's estate, Sandford Hall, in Shropshire in 1769 but died a year later, leaving his widow with four young sons. In 1766 her daughter Katherine (Kitty) married John Boyd, later a baronet, of the Boyd merchant family for whom her brother Henry had worked. Delany wrote of her delight to her niece Mary Dewes: "Were you not rejoiced to hear of Miss K. Chapone's marriage with Mr. Boyd? . . . Besides his having at least £9000 a year, he is an excellent man."[40] John Boyd was the son of Augustus Boyd who had made his fortune in the sugar plantations of the West Indies. Following the death of his first wife, Boyd married Katherine and built a Georgian Palladian villa at Danson in Bexbey designed by Robert Taylor.[41]

Delany too was widowed; following the death of Patrick Delany in 1768 she lived for part of the year in London but spent her summers at Bulstrode with her long-time friend Margaret Cavendish, Dowager Duchess of Portland, where she would begin the paper collages for which she became renowned.[42] References to her friend Sarah disappear from her correspondence and the Gloucestershire connection comes to an end. Delany took very seriously, however, her responsibilities as godmother to the Chapones' daughter Sarah. Delany had a hand in arranging her marriage to the Rev. Daniel Sandford and she remained devoted to the younger Sarah and her four sons the rest of her life. Chapone's friends John and Charles Wesley had both married, and were deeply immersed in the development of Methodism, with little lingering connection to Stanton. Only her brother Robert remained at the rectory, having succeeded his father in 1739. John Wesley recorded in his journal a rather poignant visit to the neighbourhood in December 1751. He describes a conversation with "Mr.—" (the editor assumes this to be Robert Kirkham) who attended his services in Evesham, and whose aunt "could not long forbear telling me how sorry she was that I should leave all my friends 'to lead this vagabond life.'"[43] There was little indication then of the impact that Wesley's "vagabond life" would have on the religious landscape of Britain and North America, or of the curious future of Chapone's "Essay on Laws" he had read as a young man.

The Hardships of the English Laws

Chapone's inspiration for writing and publishing a tract on the inequitable position of wives under the common law and challenging the biblical foundation of wives' subservience that underpinned it is unknown. The first surviving reference to Chapone's work appears in John Wesley's diary; Wesley's biographer Vivian Green notes that in July 1733 he is "talking in the garden, reading Varanese's papers—for she engaged in writing—and playing cards in the evening," and the following year Wesley corrected her "Essay on Laws."[44] Mary Pendarves wrote to her sister Anne in July 1734,

> I have hardly known the delight you boast of, that of having Sally's company *uninterrupted*, but next summer I promise myself something like it, if possible. The ingenious MS. was sent in my mama's box; it is an excellent piece of wit and good sense, and when *she* (the author) has rectified the *law part* of it, it will be fit for the press and the perusal of the *smartest wits of the age*.[45]

The work was published anonymously in May 1735, and there is no evidence that her authorship was publicly identified until the twentieth century.

Clearly, Astell's *Some Reflections upon Marriage* provided a model, both in approach and subject matter, but Astell had argued vigorously that women had no place in St. Stephen's Chapel (the home of the House of Commons) or in attempting to change the laws, and that the very burden of the yoke of marriage and obedience was to be submitted to with grace and a recognition that such submission was ordained by God. Chapone took a different position, arguing that submission to injustice beyond what was required by scripture was inequitable and calling on the sovereign and Parliament to rectify the law. There is no suggestion that Chapone writes out of personal grievance; her surviving letters suggests a companionable and rewarding marriage. But Chapone was a keen observer. She knew of her friend Mary's confined life as wife to Pendarves. When she writes of a wife's hopeless attempt to flee an abusive marriage, she may well have been familiar with the difficult situation of John and Charles Wesley's sister Mehetabel, married against her will to a violent husband, or of their sister Susanna whose husband, according to a letter to John from their sister Emily, beat her when she was pregnant and nearly killed her.[46] In her discussion of the use of a settlement drawn up prior to marriage to protect a wife's property, her claim that a husband is often able to circumvent this, given his legal control of her body, carries an air of authority born of experience.

She was also well informed; sources of assistance here would appear to have been her husband and her brother who had both taken degrees in civil law. John Capon had graduated B.L.L. from Trinity College, Cambridge 1725, Robert Kirkham from Merton College, Oxford B.C.L. 1735. Robert was a curate at nearby Snowshill, and succeeded his father as rector at Stanton in 1739.[47] She quotes from John Ayliffe's *A New Pandect of Roman Civil Law*, Thomas Wood's *A New Institute of the Imperial or Civil Law*, and Thomas Vernon's *Cases Argued and Adjudged in the High Court of Chancery*, as well as William Salkeld's common law *Reports of Cases adjudged in the Court of King's Bench*, suggesting that she had access either to the texts, or to notes about them. Occasionally her passages are slightly misquoted and it is possible that she is relying on manuscript notes, presumably those of her brother or husband, as it was a common practice for students to make their own copies of standard law books. The publication of *A Treatise of Feme Coverts; or, The Lady's Law* (1732) may have come to her attention at the same time that newspapers were reporting on some of the more egregious cases that figure prominently in her work. The case of Mrs. Lewis's will, for example, was reported in the *Gloucester Journal*, as was the trial of Mr. Veezy, and an account of the murder–suicide appeared in the *Gentleman's Magazine*. Chapone is careful to acknowledge her reliance on public prints when she has no better source of information.[48]

Another possible influence is *The Miseries and Great Hardships of the Inferior Clergy, in and about London* by Thomas Stackhouse (1722). It opens with the reminder that "A Complaint from the meanest Subject, express'd in Terms of Duty and Respect, finds Admittance even to the Throne of our Sovereign" and that even the meanest clergyman should not have "any Apprehensions of Danger in suing for Redress."[49] In 1731 *A Short Apology For the Common Law; Together with Proposals for Removing the Expence and Delay of Equity Proceedings* was likewise "humbly offer'd to the Consideration of Parliament, and of all Gentlemen who have a due Regard to the Civil Rights and Properties of the Subject" (London, 1731).[50] Inspiration may also have been provided by the pamphlet war occasioned by the election of 1734, particularly hard fought in the Gloucestershire region. Chapone's opening allusion to the "late Address" may allude to *The Right of British Subjects, to Petition and Apply to their Representatives, Asserted and Vindicated. In a Letter to ****** (1733). Its author insists on the historical right "by *Petition*, to inform our Kings of our Grievances," and concludes,

If then the People of *Great Britain* have a Right (and it appears this Right is undoubted) to petition the King for the sitting of Parliaments, and for the Redress of all their Grievances, it will certainly follow that they have a Right to petition a Parliament, setting forth their Hardships and Grievances.[51]

What is striking here is Chapone's adoption in her own tract of the position of the civil subject. The tradition of women petitioners dates to the civil war period and earlier, and Susan Staves, in her discussion of Catherine Macauley's account of women petitioners, notes that the Glorious Revolution's Declaration of Rights, article 5, states "That it is the right of the Subjects to petition the King and all Commitments and prosecutions for such petitioning are illegal."[52] Chapone may have modeled her self-presentation as a "Female Subject" entitled to petition the sovereign for redress on Astell's *Some Reflections*. Astell opens her Preface with an apology for her own entry in the public sphere, claiming that she "with an English Spirit and Genius, set out upon the Forlorn Hope, meaning no hurt to any body, nor designing any thing but the Publick Good, and to retrieve, if possible, the Native Liberty, the Rights and Privileges of the Subject."[53] But Astell can claim a political subject position as a *feme sole* in a way that Chapone as a wife cannot.

In their study of women, rhetoric, and the political sphere in the period, Jennifer Richards and Alison Thorne observe that religion and scripture would come to empower women in ways that helped compensate for their exclusion from the humanist education curriculum and its training in rhetoric that prepared the student for public life. One strategy was to employ "familial or domestic identities to speak or write of matters that exceeded the confines of domestic life," and the authors trace the tradition of the genre or mode of "supplication and complaint" for women's public expression, which makes Chapone's bold statement by contrast so extraordinary.[54] The second part of her text addresses "the Original Curse of Subjection passed upon the Woman" and coming as it does after the powerfully persuasive analysis of the law, the finely honed argument and incisive logic falters a little. Like Astell, Chapone fully accepts the biblical account of creation and the consequences that have put wives in subjection to their husbands; the only mitigation she can offer is the belief that men and women would have been equal prior to the Fall, so that inequality is a temporary sublunary state, and in any case, the harshness of the English common law far exceeds any reasonable restrictions countenanced by scripture.

Although *The Hardships of the English Laws* was published anonymously, the attribution to Chapone is well supported. Anna Hopkins writes to George Ballard on December 14, 1741,

I am sorry it is not in my power to send you Mrs Astell's Proposal to the Ladies. I borrow'd it of Mrs Chapon, and sent it home long ago, but I dare say she will very willingly lend it you. Tho' I knew that she was the Author of Hardships of English Laws &c; I did not mention it to you because I thought it was a secret.[55]

In a letter dated June 11, 1743, Ballard's friend Thomas Rawlins mentions that remarks on "Mrs. Chapon's Book intituled ye Hardships" were published in the *Gentleman's Magazine*, and a month later he mentions seeing someone at Ragley who "promised me that I shd be obliged with the Book intituled ye Hardships of the English Laws & because it is not to be met with in London" and offers to transcribe the comments.[56]

The Hardships of the English Laws appeared in May 1735 with editions in London, printed by James Roberts, and Dublin, printed by George Faulkner, and excerpts were published in the May and June issues of the *Gentleman's Magazine*.[57] The Bowyer Ledgers indicate that a print order for 750 copies May 12 of *The Hardships* came from "the Rev. Mr. Seward."[58] The "Rev. Mr. Seward" remains unidentified. William Seward (1711–1740), brother of Benjamin mentioned earlier, was not ordained, although his public role with the Methodists could easily account for the error. His brother Thomas (1708–1790) became "the Rev. Mr. Seward" and according to Samuel Pegge was a friend of both Elstob and Chapone, but Teresa Barnard notes that following his ordination in 1731 he was sent to a rectory in Wales that he left in 1735 to join the household of the Duke of Grafton at Euston House in Suffolk as tutor to the second son, so a visit to the Bowyer print shop remains only a slight possibility. In his study of the Bowyer ledgers, Keith Maslen writes that one avenue for distribution for self-published authors, at least for short works such as "a controversial pamphlet or a single sermon," was to use a bookseller such as "Roberts or the Coopers, who specialized in pamphlets."[59] John Wesley may have assisted with the printing and distribution of the tract, for at the time he was assisting Bowyer in the printing of his father Samuel Wesley's *Dissertationes in Librum Jobi*, a lengthy commentary on Job published the following year, and he also published his own *A Sermon preached at St. Mary's in Oxford, On Sunday, September 21, 1735*, sold by James Roberts. The tract was advertised in the London papers, including the *Daily Journal*, *Weekly Miscellany*, *London Evening Post*, and *New Grub Street Journal*. In the fall of 1736 two letters, one particularly critical, were published in the *Weekly Miscellany*, and the following summer its editor, the Rev. William Webster, published his own letter to the anonymous author of *The Hardships of the English Laws* together with her reply (see Appendix One). His letter proposing that she contribute to the *Miscellany* and her reply suggest both admiration on the editor's part for Chapone's abilities and a reluctance on Chapone's part that she attributes to her domestic cares. References to *The Hardships of the English Laws* disappear, but the arguments Chapone advanced would return in a more oblique form in the novels appearing by mid-century, and the conversations they generated.

Remarks on Mrs. Muilman's Letter to the Right Honourable the Earl of Chesterfield. In a Letter to Mrs. Muilman

On December 27, 1750, shortly after the commencement of her correspondence with Samuel Richardson, Chapone wrote from Cheltenham to George Ballard and mentions Richardson, who "has honrd us with his friendship and correspondence," and relays his offer to assist Ballard with his book on eminent women of Britain. She rather ingenuously adds, in reference to the women who had recently published their scandalous memoirs,

> one of them has met with a Rebuke, from one of her own Sex. It is entitled, An Answer to, and some Remarks upon Mrs. Muilman's. . . . I desire you will read it, and give me your opinion of it. Tho' as it has made some noise, I suppose you may have seen it already. I fancy it will suit your taste.[60]

"Mrs. Muilman" was the courtesan Constantia Phillips, who by her early teens had been seduced and then had embarked on a life made notorious by a number of marriages and liaisons. Her second marriage, to Henry Muilman in 1724, ended soon after when he sued for an annulment. The ensuing legal battles continued for decades and became the stuff of legal legend. At one point, when the case appeared to be about to conclude, the judge was about to pronounce sentence when Muilman's lawyer "threw upon the table an appeal to the Court of Arches." The judge, Dr. Humphry Henchman, was so angry that he offered Phillips "his services, free of charge, as one of her legal counsel, a service he continued to perform until his death in 1739."[61] A life of extravagance and a series of lovers had left her in poverty by the late 1740s, and when the threat of publishing her memoir failed to generate any funds from the men she hoped to embarrass, she proceeded with publication of her memoir, and her side of the legal dispute, *An Apology for the Conduct of Mrs. Teresia Constantia Phillips, more Particularly that Part of it which relates to her Marriage with an Eminent Dutch Merchant*, in 1748. The three-volume publication was printed for the author, and sold from Phillips's house, each copy individually signed to assure authentication (and because, she claimed, no bookseller would sell it). The writer Paul Whitehead has been credited with writing some or all of the work, but the entry for Phillips in the *Orlando* entry is clear about the woman's voice in the text.[62] Lynda M. Thompson's study of the women who became known as the "scandalous memoirists" argues persuasively that Phillips turned to publication as a means of creating a property, and a sense of self, from the narrative of her life and her ordeal, and that this self-assertion from such a woman was as shocking to her readers as her public accounts of her numerous affairs.[63]

Phillips followed up her book with a pamphlet published two years later, in London and Dublin 1750, *A Letter Humbly Address'd to the Right Honourable The Earl of Chesterfield*. The statesman and man of letters Philip Stanhope, Fourth Earl of Chesterfield, was an acquaintance—possibly more—of Phillips and in the *Letter* she defends her *Memoirs* and the decision to publish them to him, outlining in detail the labyrinthine legal procedures that had blocked her efforts to obtain justice in the courts and vigorously protesting the legal and social double standards that left her as a woman disgraced and impoverished while the men responsible continued to sin with impunity, their social standing unimpaired.

Chapone wrote and published a response to this letter, *Remarks on Mrs. Muilman's Letter to the Right Honourable the Earl of Chesterfield. In a Letter to*

Mrs. Muilman. The text was printed by Richardson and sold by William Owen in London, and James Leake (Richardson's brother-in-law) in Bath. There is no obvious explanation for Chapone's decision to respond in print, although the scandal memoirs were met with widespread condemnation, and Phillips's attempt to further defend her life and her act of publication may have provoked Chapone, perhaps with some encouragement, to offer her "rebuke." One of the few surviving comments on Chapone's *Remarks* is from Elizabeth Montagu, who had already detected the influence of Chapone's reading. "There is a pamphlet," she writes, "which amuses me, (by a lady,) addressed to Mrs. Con. Philips, and designed as an answer to her letter to Lord Chesterfield; it is written with some spirit and argument, but it has the female frailty of displaying more learning than is necessary or graceful." Montagu goes on to suggest that perhaps too much reading of *Clarissa* has "spoiled her style by an imitation of Mr. Richardson."[64] Chapone was indeed a very keen reader of Richardson's novel, but Montagu's remark raises the possibility that Richardson had a hand in editing as well as printing Chapone's *Remarks.*[65]

Chapone in her response sympathizes with the abuses and miseries that marked Phillips's early life, but soon moves on to condemn her attempts to justify the deliberate choices that led inevitably to ruin, to reject the remorse over consequences rather than moral behavior, and ultimately to dismiss any plea for forgiveness and pardon not founded on Christian contrition. Claire Brant observes that while women rarely had the financial resources to deploy the law for redress, "women's charges against socially more powerful men could win conviction in texts as they could not in courts."[66] Chapone may have been piqued to see another woman attack in print the disadvantages for women under England's law, but in this case employed in such disgraceful cause; good women were entitled in equity to equal treatment, whereas bad women should not blame their woes on the legal system.

* * *

The Hardships of the English Laws reproduces on its title page several passages of biblical scripture, concluding with lines from Psalm 55. We cannot know if these were suggested by Chapone herself, or added at the print shop. The lines from the psalmist lamenting the betrayal by "thou, a man, mine Equal, my Guide, and mine Acquaintance" perhaps seemed apropos to someone who had only a slight knowledge of the contents. Chapone of course would have known the psalm, but would have been equally familiar with the Church of England's *Book of Common Prayer.* There, the same Psalm opens with, "Hear my prayer, O God: and hide not thy self from my petition."[67] Sarah Chapone had thought long and deeply, read carefully, and observed astutely. Later in life she would enter into an intensely engaged correspondence with the novelist Samuel Richardson about the position of women in England and the legal status of the main character of his novel *Clarissa.* While strongly influenced by the Cartesian philosophy and fearless rhetorical style of the philosopher Mary Astell, Chapone's arguments were her own. Despite her obvious admiration for Astell, Chapone parted company when it came to her response to those inequities for married women Astell had so clearly limned. Chapone identified them instead as injustices to be rectified, and her response was to produce a polemic in the form of a petition to Parliament and the sovereign on behalf of all English wives. In it she argues eloquently and persuasively that, even given the lesser status of wives who are under the biblical injunction to submit to their husbands, the laws of England impose inequities and penalties far in excess of anything warranted by scripture, and that an English government under a sovereign committed to the liberties and rights of the subject has a duty to remedy this injustice.

In his reflection on why the written history of the law in England remains incomplete, John Baker reminds his readers that there is a world of law outside the courtroom, and that to focus on the legal cases that reach the courts is to neglect that world of law that exists "in the sense that people are aware of it and conform to it, even when it is neither written down in legislation nor the subject of accessible declarations by the judiciary."[68] The common law had grown into being as an accretion of centuries of practice, precedent, rulings, judgments, and statutes, and was shaped and grounded in narrative: the formality of the writs and precedents recorded in the yearbooks and written reports were daily given life in the pleadings and judgments of oral practice. Yet the law is not "unwritten," and a vast archive of speaking the law moved to paper and to new forms of cultural expression. Chapone's *Hardships of the English Laws in Relation to Wives* provides not only a window into one area of the law outside the courtroom, but forms part of the documentary record of women's coming into legal personhood.

Notes

1 "A Tract on the Unreasonableness of the Law in Regard to Wives," *The Columbian Magazine*, May 1788, p. 245, 246. *Google Books*.
2 Ruth Perry, review of *Women Writers and the Early Modern British Political Tradition*, ed. Hilda Smith, *American Historical Review* 105, no. 1 (Feb. 2000): 276–278.
3 There is an extensive body of scholarship on women and the law in the early modern period. For England in the eighteenth century see especially Joanne Bailey, "Favoured or Oppressed? Married Women, Property and 'Coverture' in England, 1660–1800," *Continuity and Change* 17, no. 3 (2002): 351–372; Amy Erickson, *Women and Property in Early Modern England* (New York: Routledge, 1995); Lynne A. Greenberg, Introduction to *Legal Treatises. Essential Works for the Study of Early Modern Women, Series III, Part One*, vol. 1 (Farnham, Surrey: Ashgate, 2005), ix–lxiii; Rebecca Probert, *Marriage Law and Practice in the Long Eighteenth Century: A Reassessment* (Cambridge: Cambridge University Press, 2009); Susan Staves, *Married Women's Separate Property in England, 1660–1833* (Cambridge, MA: Harvard University Press, 1990); Tim Stretton, "Coverture and Unity of Person in Blackstone's *Commentaries*," in *Blackstone and his* Commentaries: *Biography, Law, History*, ed. Wilfrid Prest (Oxford: Hart, 2009): 111–127; Tim Stretton and Krista J. Kesselring, eds., *Married Women and the Law: Coverture in England and the Common Law World* (Montreal: McGill-Queen's Press, 2013); Nancy E. Wright, Margaret W. Ferguson, and A. R. Buck, eds., *Women, Property, and the Letters of the Law in Early Modern England* (Toronto: University of Toronto Press, 2004).

4 Stanton with Snowshill Parish Records, TS 1572–1734/35, Gloucestershire Public Record Office, Gloucester, England. Chapone is referred to here as Sarah until her marriage, and Chapone thereafter.

5 Robert Atkyns, *The Ancient and Present State of Glostershire* (London, 1712), 684–685, Eighteenth Century Collections Online, cited hereafter as ECCO; V. H. H. Green, *The Young Mr. Wesley: A Study of John Wesley and Oxford* (London: Edward Arnold, 1961), 205.

6 Susan Staves, "Church of England Clergy and Women Writers," *Huntington Library Quarterly* 65, no. 1/2 (2002): 81.

7 Mary Delany, *The Autobiography and Correspondence of Mary Granville, Mrs. Delany*, ed. Lady Llanover, vol. 1 (London, 1861), 15, 16 (cited hereafter as *Correspondence* with year and volume). In her adulthood Mary Granville will be identified by her surname; first Granville, then Pendarves following her first marriage, then Delany following her second marriage.

8 For details about Delany's life see Mark Laird and Alicia Weisberg-Roberts, eds., *Mrs. Delany & Her Circle* (New Haven, CT: Yale Center for British Art, Yale University Press, 2009); Ruth Hayden, *Mrs. Delany, Her Life and Her Flowers* (New York: New Amsterdam, 1992).

9 Mary Pendarves to Anne Granville, April 16, 1728. *Correspondence* (1861) 1.167.

10 Mary Pendarves to Anne Granville 4 Jan. 1736–1737. *Correspondence* (1861) 1.586.

11 See Henry D. Rack, *Reasonable Enthusiast: John Wesley and the Rise of Methodism*, 3rd ed. (London: Epworth Press, 2002), 61–106.

12 Wesley, Susanna. *Susanna Wesley: The Complete Writings*, ed. Charles Wallace, Jr. (New York: Oxford University Press, 1997), 132.

13 Elizabeth Elstob to Anne Granville, August 4, 1739. *Correspondence*, (1861), 2.57.

14 Michael McDonnell, *The Registers of St. Paul's School 1509–1748* (London: Privately Printed for the Governors, 1977), 395, 400.

15 Norma Clarke, "Elizabeth Elstob (1674–1752): England's First Professional Woman Historian?" *Gender & History* 17, no. 1 (2005), 218.

16 Mary Pendarves to Anne Granville, October 15, 1730. *Correspondence* (1861), 1:263–264.

17 For further discussion see Susan Paterson Glover, "Further Reflections upon Marriage: Mary Astell and Sarah Chapone," in *Feminist Interpretations of Mary Astell*, eds. (Alice Sowaal and Penny Weiss, University Park, PA: Penn State University Press, 2016), 93–108; Jocelyn Harris's "Philosophy and Sexual Politics in Mary Astell and Samuel Richardson," *Intellectual History Review* 22, no. 3 (2012): 445–463.

18 For a discussion of changes made to the 1730 edition of *Some Reflections upon Marriage* (1730) and Samuel Richardson's possible role see John Dussinger, "Mary Astell's Revisions of *Some Reflections upon Marriage* (1730)," *The Papers of the Bibliographical Society of America* 107, no. 1 (2013): 49–79.

19 Sarah Chapone to George Ballard, Dowdeswell March 12, 1741/2. Ballard MS 43 fol.132.

20 "Bernardus Utopiensis," *A Second Dissertation on the Liberty of Preaching Granted to Women by the People called Quakers* (Dublin, 1739). ECCO.

21 Sarah Chapone to Mrs. Knightly, April 24, 1736. Letters of Sarah Chapone, vol. D2383/F14.3.

22 For an analysis of the epistolary exchange in the Ballard correspondence see Leonie Hannan, "Collaborative Scholarship on the Margins: An Epistolary Network," *Women's Writing* 21, no. 3, 2014: 290–315.

23 Ruth Perry, Introduction, *Memoirs of Several Learned Ladies of Great Britain*, by George Ballard (Wayne State University Press, 1985), 21.

24 Sarah Chapone to George Ballard, July 3, 1749. Ballard MS 43 fol.147.

25 Mary Pendarves to Anne Granville, January 24, 1732/3. *Correspondence* 1861, 1:395.

26 Patricia Springborg suggests *The Arguments of Mons. Herard for the Duke of Mazarin against the Dutchess, his Spouse, and the Factum for the dutchess by Mons. St.*

Evremont (1699), cited in her edition of Mary Astell, *Some Reflections upon Marriage in Astell: Political Writings* (Cambridge: Cambridge University Press, 1996), 7 n.1 (cited hereafter as *Some Reflections*); Ruth Perry suggests "the duchess's autobiographical *Mémoires D'Hortense et de Marie Mancini* (1676)," *The Celebrated Mary Astell: An Early English Feminist* (Chicago, IL: University of Chicago Press, 1986), 153. For additional discussion see *"The Wandering Life I Led"*: *Essays on Hortense Mancini, Duchess Mazarin and Early Modern Women's Border Crossings*, eds. Susan Shifrin (Newcastle upon Tyne, UK: Cambridge Scholars Publishing, 2009).

27 T. C. Duncan Eaves and Ben D. Kimpel, *Samuel Richardson: A Biography* (Oxford: Clarendon, 1971), 351.

28 Sarah Chapone to Samuel Richardson, Cheltenham October 12, 1750. Forster and Dyce Collections, Part Two: 18th Century Manuscripts. *Papers of Samual Richardson* (Harvester Press Microform Publications, 1986), Reel 15.126, F.48.E.6 (cited hereafter as *Richardson Papers*). A new edition of Samuel Richardson's correspondence is currently in preparation at Cambridge University Press under the editorial direction of Thomas Keymer and Peter Sabor.

29 Samuel Richardson to Sarah Chapone December 6, 1750. *Richardson Papers*, Reel 15. F.48.E.6 Item 128.

30 Sarah Chapone to Samuel Richardson February 25, 1750/51. *Richardson Papers*, Reel 15. F.48.E.6 Item 133.

31 Samuel Richardson, *Selected Letters of Samuel Richardson*, ed. John Carroll (Oxford: Clarendon, 1964), 25.

32 For discussion of this exchange, see Clarissa Campbell Orr, "The Sappho of Gloucestershire," in *Bluestockings Now!: The Evolution of a Social Role*, ed. Deborah Heller, Farnham, UK: Ashgate, 2015: 91–110.

33 Eaves and Kimpel, 354.

34 Sarah Chapone to George Ballard, December 11, 1752 in Ballard MS 43 fol. 174; Sarah Chapone to George Ballard, January 21, 1753 in Ballard MS 43 fol. 180; Sarah Chapone to George Ballard, January 25, 1753 in Ballard MS 43 fol. 183.

35 Sarah Chapone to Mrs. Norwood, October 20, 1752, in *Richardson Papers*, Reel 15. F.48.E.6 Item 150.

36 Mary Delany to Anne Dewes, November 5, 1754. *Correspondence* (1861) 3:299.

37 Mary Delany to Anne Dewes, December 28, 1760. *Correspondence* (1861) 3:624.

38 On Richardson see Thomas Keymer, *Richardson's 'Clarissa' and the Eighteenth-Century Reader* (Cambridge: Cambridge University Press, 1992, 2004), 103. Richardson's side of the correspondence has not survived, but Mulso's letters were published after her death in *The Posthumous Works of Mrs. Chapone. Containing her Correspondence with Mr. Richardson, A Series of Letters to Mrs. Elizabeth Carter, and Some Fugitive Pieces, Never Before Published*, vol. 2 (London, 1807). For an introduction to this work see Barbara Eaton, *Yes, Papa! Mrs. Chapone and the Bluestocking Circle: A Biography of Hester Mulso—Mrs. Chapone (1727–1801), a Bluestocking* (London: Francis Boutle, 2012), 47–59; Betty Schellenberg, *Literary Coteries and the Making of Modern Print Culture 1740–1790* (Cambridge: Cambridge University Press, 2016), 33–59; and Laura E. Thomason, *The Matrimonial Trap: Eighteenth-Century Women Writers Redefine Marriage* (Lewisburg: Bucknell University Press, 2014), chap. 3.

39 Hester Chapone to Elizabeth Carter February 4, 1761, *The Posthumous Works of Mrs. Chapone*, vol. 1 (London: John Murray, 1807), 122.

40 Mary Delany to Mary Dewes n.d. 1776. *Correspondence* (1862) 1:81.

41 See Richard Lea and Chris Miele with Gordon Higgott, *Danson House: The Anatomy of a Georgian Villa* (Swindon, UK: English Heritage, 2011), 7. The house was recently restored to its Georgian origins by English Heritage and is open for public view.

42 For a detailed examination of her paper collage work, with illustrations, see Laird and Weisberg-Roberts, *Mrs. Delany & Her Circle*.

43 John Wesley, *The Works of John Wesley*, vol. 20, Journal and Diaries III (1743–1754), ed. W. Reginald Ward and Richard P. Heitzenrater (Nashville, TN: Abingdon Press, 1991), 412.

44 Green, 224, 294, n.1.

45 Mary Pendarves to Anne Granville, July 22, 1734. *Correspondence* (1861) 1:486–87.

46 See Emily Wesley to John Wesley February 9, 1729/30, Wesley Family Papers, DDWF/6/3.

47 See the Clergy of the Church of England Database, s.v. "Robert Kirkham."

48 For the Lewis case see the *Gloucester Journal*, February 27, 1732–33; for the Veezy trial February 1, 1731–32. For the murder–suicide see the *Gentleman's Magazine*, April 1732.

49 Thomas Stackhouse, *The Miseries and Great Hardships of the Inferior Clergy, in and about London. And a modest plea for the rights, and better usage; in a Letter to the Right Reverend Father in God, John Lord Bishop of London* (London, 1722), 1–2. ECCO.

50 *A Short Apology For the Common Law; Together with Proposals for Removing the Expence and Delay of Equity Proceedings* (London, 1731), t.p. ECCO.

51 *The Right of British Subjects, to Petition and Apply to their Representatives, Asserted and Vindicated. In a Letter to ****** (London, 1733), 6, 16. ECCO.

52 Susan Staves, "'The Liberty of a She-Subject of England': Rights Rhetoric and the Female Thucydides," *Cardozo Studies in Law and Literature* 1, no. 2 (1989): 165. See also Bernard Capp, "Separate Domains? Women and Authority in Early Modern England," in *The Experience of Authority in Early Modern England*, eds. Paul Griffiths, Adam Fox, and Steve Hindle (Basingstoke, UK: Macmillan, 1996), 117–145; Patricia Crawford and Sara Mendelson, *Women in Early Modern England* (Oxford: Clarendon, 1998), Patricia Crawford and Laura Gowing, eds., *Women's Worlds in Seventeenth-Century England: A Sourcebook* (London: Routledge, 2000), chap. 9; and Paula Backscheider, "Hanging on and Hanging in: Women's Struggle to Participate in Public Sphere Debate," in *Everyday Revolutions: Eighteenth-Century Women Transforming Public and Private*, eds. Diane E. Boyd and Marta Kvande (Newark, DE: University of Delaware Press, 2008), 30–66.

53 Astell, *Some Reflections*, 8.

54 Jennifer Richards and Alison Thorne, Introduction to *Rhetoric, Women and Politics in Early Modern England* (London: Routledge, 2007), 14. For an analysis of Chapone's concept of liberty see Jacqueline Broad, "'A Great Championess for her Sex': Sarah Chapone on Liberty as Nondomination and Self-Mastery," *The Monist* 98, no. 1 (2015): 77–88.

55 Anna Hopkins to George Ballard, December 14, 1741, Ballard MS 43 fol. 106.

56 Thomas Rawlins to George Ballard, June 11, 1743. Ballard MS 41 fol. 238; Thomas Rawlins to George Ballard, July 12, 1743. Ballard MS 41 fol. 239.

57 *Gentleman's Magazine*, May 1735, 241–242; June 1735, 284.

58 Keith Maslen and John Lancaster, eds., *The Bowyer Ledgers: The Printing Accounts of William Bowyer, Father and Son, reproduced on Microfiche: With a Checklist of Bowyer Printing, 1699–1777, a Commentary, Indexes, and Appendixes* (London: The Bibliographical Society, 1991), 170.

59 Samuel Pegge, *An Historical Account of that Venerable Monument of Antiquity the Textus Roffensis; including Memoirs of the Learned Saxonists Mr. William Elstob and his Sister* (London, 1784), 28, ECCO; Teresa Barnard, *Anna Seward: A Constructed Life: A Critical Biography* (Farnham, UK: Ashgate, 2009), 26; Keith Maslen, *An Early London Printing House at Work: Studies in the Bowyer Ledgers. With a Supplement to The Bowyer Ornament Stock (1973), an appendix on the Bowyer-Emonson partnership, and 'Bowyer's Paper Stock Ledger'*, by Herbert Davis (New York: The Bibliographical Society of America, 1993), 99.

60 Sarah Chapone to George Ballard, December 27, 1750. Ballard MS 43 fol. 155.

61 Lawrence Stone, *Uncertain Unions: Marriage in England, 1660–1753* (Oxford: Oxford University Press, 1992), 265.

62 *Orlando: Women's Writing in the British Isles from the Beginnings to the Present*, s.v. "Constantia Phillips."

63 Lynda M. Thompson, *The "Scandalous Memoirists": Constantia Phillips, Laetitia Pilkington and the Shame of "Publick Fame"* (Manchester, UK: Manchester University Press, 2000). Caroline Breashears discusses the problematic generic limitations of the term "scandalous memoirs" for a range of disparate texts in "Scandalous Categories: Classifying the Memoirs of Unconventional Women," *Philological Quarterly* 82, no. 2 (2003): 187–212. On Pilkington and Phillips see Norma Clarke, *Queen of the Wits: A Life of Laetitia Pilkington* (London, Faber and Faber, 2008), Daniel Cook, "An Authoress to be Let," in *Women's Life Writing, 1700–1850: Gender, Genre and Authorship*, eds. Daniel Cook and Amy Culley (Houndmills, UK: Palgrave Macmillan, 2012), 39–54; and Victoria Joule, "'Heroines of their own Romance': Creative Exchanges between Life-Writing and Fiction, the 'Scandalous Memoirists' and Charlotte Lennox," *Journal for Eighteenth-Century Studies* 37, no. 1 (2014): 37–52.

64 Elizabeth Montagu, *Letters of Mrs. E. Montagu, with some of the Letters of her Correspondence*, vol. 3 (London: Cadell and Davies, 1813), 134–135.

65 For a discussion of Richardson's practice of editing works he printed see Dussinger, 54–59.

66 Clare Brant, "Speaking of Women: Scandal and the Law in the Mid-Eighteenth Century," *Women, Texts and Histories 1575–1760*, eds. Clare Brant and Diane Purkiss (London: Routledge, 1992), 261.

67 *The Book of Common Prayer, and Administration of the Sacraments, And Other Rites and Ceremonies of the Church, according to the use of the Church of England: together with the Psalter Of David, Pointed as they are to be sung or said in Churches*, London, 1731: n.p. ECCO.

68 J. H. Baker, "Why the History of English Law Has Not Been Finished," *Cambridge Law Journal* 59, no.1 (2000): 78–79.

Part One

The Hardships of the English Laws in Relation to Wives.

With an Explanation of the Original Curse of Subjection passed upon the Woman.

In an Humble Address to the Legislature.

The Hardships of the *English* Laws in Relation to Wives.

With an Explanation of the Original Curse of Subjection passed upon the Woman.

In an Humble Address to the Legislature.

---

*I could also speak as ye do; if your Soul were in my Souls Stead,
I could* heap up Words against you, and shake mine Head at you.
But I would strengthen you with my Mouth, and the moving of my
Lips should asswage your Grief.
Tho' I speak, my Grief is not asswaged; and tho' I forbear, what am
I eased? *Job. xvi. 4, 5, 6.*
*For it was not an Enemy that reproached me, then I could have born
it;* neither was it he that hated me, that did magnifie himself
against me, then I would have hid my self from him.
But it was thou, a Man, mine Equal, my Guide, and mine Acquaint-
ance.
We took sweet Counsel together, and walked into the House of God
in Company. *Psalm. lvi. 12, 13, 14.*[1]

London,

Printed by W. Bowyer, for J. Roberts, at the *Oxford*
Arms in Warwick Lane. *MDCCXXXV.*

(*Price one Shilling.*)

The CONTENTS.

The Hardships of the *English* Laws in Relation to Wives.

IN a late Address made to his Majesty by a very ingenious Writer, he presumes upon the Privilege of the Free-born Subjects of *England* to approach their Sovereign, represent their Grievances, and humbly to implore Redress.

[2] We hope that this inestimable Privilege is not wholly confined to the *Male* Line, but that we his Majesty's faithful *Female* Subjects, may also shelter ourselves under his most gracious Protection, our Condition being of all others in his Dominions the most deplorable, we being the least able to help ourselves, and the most exposed to Oppression.

This is certainly true, in every State of Life, but in none so notoriously, and without all Redress, as when we put ourselves in a Condition of adding to his Majesty's Subjects by becoming *Wives*, under which Character we humbly address his most sacred Majesty, and the honourable Houses of Parliament, for an Alteration or a Repeal of some Laws, which, as we conceive, put us in a worse Condition than *Slavery* itself.

We are now apprehensive of more frequent Oppression from these Laws, as this is an Age in which the Foundation of all the noble Principles of Christianity (which are our only Protection) are broken up, and *Deism*, that Underminer of all that is truly laudable, with its Legions of Immorality, Prophaneness, and consummate Impudence are let in upon us.

[3] All religious Truths may, and ought to be the Subject of an humble and modest Enquiry; but are by no Means, the proper Objects of Ridicule and Contempt. But since some Men by their extraordinary Flights of Conceit have thought fit to assail the Almighty, and are endeavouring to bring over the rest of their Sex, as fast as they can, 'tis Time for Us to look about us, and to use all justifiable Methods to provide against the impending Danger: For since we seem to be hastening into a *State* of *Nature*, in which there can be no Appeal but to the Laws of our Country, and the Authority of Scripture is going down, which directs a Man to erect a private *Court* of *Equity* in his own Breast, what shall restrain the *Strong* from oppressing the *Weak*, if the Laws of our Country do not, they being in such a State the only established Rules of Society?³

I humbly hope therefore, that this will not be thought an unseasonable Representation of our Condition, since supposing a Man no Christian, he may be as *Despotick* (excepting the Power over Life itself) as the Grand Seignior in his Seraglio, with this Difference only, that the *English* Husband has but *one Vassal* to treat according to his variable Humour, whereas the Grand Seignior having *many*, it may be supposed, [4] that some of them, at some Times may be suffered to be at quiet.

What our Fate will be God only knows, if the present Wits of the Age should be attended with Success, and strengthened by Numbers. As for Arguments they are out of the Question with them, their Weapons being *Points* of *Wit*, *Smart Jests*, and *all-confounding Laughter*. These they brandish about against Heaven or Earth, as they happen to oppose their Wills and Inclinations, which stand with them for Reason and Religion.

If therefore we may claim the Privilege of *English* Subjects to speak our Grievances, and be indulged with a gracious Attention, the following Particulars, contain the chief Articles of our Complaint.

I. That the Estate of Wives is more disadvantagious than *Slavery* itself.

II. That Wives may be made Prisoners for Life at the Discretion of their *Domestick Governors*, whose Power, as we at Present apprehend, bears no Manner of Proportion to that Degree of Authority, which is vested in any other Set of Men in *England*. For though the Legislature, acting collectively, may dispose of Life and Fortune; no indi- [5] vidual, not even the Sovereign himself, can *imprison* any Person for *Life*, at *Will* and *Pleasure*; the *Habeas Corpus* Act, providing for the Condemnation or Enlargement of the Prisoner.

III. That Wives have no Property, neither in their *own Persons, Children,* or *Fortunes*.

I grant the Laws I presume to complain of, gratify some Mens *Pride*, fall in with their *Interest*, and oblige their *Humours*; that they will be very loath to part with them, and that they can plead *Prescription* for them. But I deny that they are reasonable or just. All which I shall endeavour to prove,

By Facts, and

By Observations upon them.

Case I. The first Case I cite, was lately determined in the Court of Delegates in Doctor's Commons, relating to the Will of one Mrs. *Lewis* a Widow. While she was in that State she made a Will; soon after she married again; in some time her second Husband died, and she again became a Widow, without any Children by either Husband. The Will which she made in her first Widowhood remaining, and being found after her Death, the Question was, whether it was [6] a good Will or not? The Council for the Will cited many Authorities from the civil Law, and shewed, that among the *Romans*, if a Man had made his Will, and was afterwards taken *Captive*, such Will *revived* and became again in Force, by the Testator's repossessing his *Liberty*: And thence inferred, that as Marriage was a *State* of *Captivity*, Wills made by Women who became *Free* by Survivorship ought to *revive* with their Freedom.

But the Court finding one Distinction, *viz.* that Marriage was a *voluntary* Act, and Captivity the Effect of *Compulsion*, the Judges determined the Will to be void.

Observation, The Arguments of the Council make the Estate of Wives *equal* to, the Distinction of the Court *worse* than, Slavery itself.

Case II. An unfortunate Wife who had been so cruelly treated by her Husband, that Life itself was became a Burthen to her, at last made her Application to her Brother, who was a Clergy-Man, and inclined by all the Motives of Christianity to assist her. He received her into his House, with her Spirit quite opprest and sunk by her Husband's Severity, which had so far affected her Constitution, that she was in a very bad State of Health. He went to her Husband, and [7] in the softest Terms represented his unmanly Treatment of his Wife, and the sad Effects it had had upon her; and endeavour'd, by all possible Arguments, to awaken in his Mind some Sentiments of common Humanity towards her; adding, that (with his *Leave*) she should be welcome to stay at his House, till she had recovered her Health, of which he would be at the sole Expense. But alass! how unavailing is Reason, and soft Persuasion, when opposed to *Insolent Power*, and *Arbitrary Will*. The Husband insisted upon his *Right* to *controul*; it was an Invasion of his *Prerogative Royal* for his Wife to pretend to expostulate, and in short he ordered her Brother to send her Home again, or keep her at his *Peril*. This was the unhappy Creature's last Effort; and this ill Success, flung her into a lingering *Fever*, of which she languished a Fortnight, when her Husband came in Person, and demanded his Wife. Her Brother was forced to deliver her up, being as unable to contend with her Husband, as the Senator of *Rome* with the Emperor, when he declared he was never ashamed to give up an Argument to a Man, who was master of fifty Legions. Thus the miserable Wife was carried Home again, where her Husband, exasperated by her Complaint, treated her with greater Harshness, [8] which gave her, her *Coup de Grace* in less than a Month; when she left her Sufferings to be avenged by Heaven, though they were disregarded by Men, from whom she could find no Redress, her Husband never having beaten her, nor threatened her Life, though he took all other Methods to break her Heart.

Case III. The next Case I shall relate is very short, consisting of few Particulars. A young Lady possest of a considerable Fortune in Land and Money, married a Gentleman, in whom she had such full Trust and Confidence, that she made no Reserve to herself, but flung her whole Fortune with her Person entirely into his Power. As he had no Fortune of his own, it was a fine thing to him to be master of an Estate; he launched out into the most extravagant Expences, but soon finding some Frugality necessary, he thought fit to *confine* his Wife in her Country House, with the bare Allowance of the necessary Supports of Life, and one Servant to attend her, who was also her Jailer. In this Confinement she lived, till it pleased that Being, who *alone* had *Power*, to set her *Free*.

Case IV. The next Instance I shall produce, is the Case of Mr. *Veezey*, tryed at the *Old Bailey*, where it was proved that he con- [9] fined his Wife for some Years in a Garret, without Fire, proper Cloathing, or any of the Comforts of Life; that he had frequently Horse-whipt her; that her Sufferings were so great and intolerable, that she destroyed her wretched Life by flinging herself out at the Window.

But as there was Bread found in the Room, which, though hard and mouldy, was supposed sufficient to sustain Life; and as it was not thought that he pushed her out at the Window himself, he was acquitted, and that Complaint of her Sufferings served only to instruct Husbands in the full Extent of their despotick Power.

Observation, From these three Cases it appears that Husbands have a more *Afflictive* Power than that of *Life* and *Death*.

About five Years ago, a modest agreeable Gentlewoman, well educated, married a young Tradesman, he set up with a good Fortune of his and hers, and in three Years Time, by his Vices, Extravagancies, and Follies, ran it out every farthing. Upon which he flung himself into the Army, in the Condition of a common foot Soldier.

She then desired his Permission to serve a Lady of Quality, by which Means she hoped to be able to provide for their two Children. But he refused it, unless he might [10] have leave to visit her, when he pleased; and the Wages which she should earn, being his not hers, unless it was paid to him, he might have sued the Person, who should entertain her. This effectually barred the Doors against her as a Servant. If by the Kindness of Friends she should be enabled to take an House, and set up in any Way of Business to maintain herself and helpless Infants, it would be only giving him an Opportunity to *Plunder* her at *Discretion*.

The last Resource in such a Case is, to transact her Business in another's Name. But it is very difficult to find a Friend generous enough to involve himself in the intricate Affairs of an helpless undone Woman, who may be commanded from the Place and Employment, at the Pleasure of her Lord and Master, against whose Injunctions she can make no Appeal. The most that her Friends can do, is to afford her a small Pittance by Stealth in the Nature of an Alms, by which she may be sometimes relieved, but never provided for, unless they were in Condition to settle an Estate in Trustees Hands for her Use, which (considering the Power the Husband has over her Person) he may soon convert to his own.

[11] *Observation*, Hence it appears, that Wives have no Property neither in their intellectual, or personal Abilities, nor in their Fortunes.

When we look back into the Annals of Queen *Mary* I. we Shrink with Horror at the Apprehension of her Fire and Faggot. But behold! the Sufferings which an Husband may inflict upon his Free-born *English* Wife, if he so please; and then consider which of the fiery Tryals are the more tolerable!

If we cannot in Justice call for the Correction of these Tyrannies, we hope we may in Charity for the Prevention of them.

I must here take Notice, that I have related the Case of Mrs. *Veezey*, as I found it in one of the publick Prints, I therefore don't take upon my self to say that this Case is truly stated, 'tis possible some material Circumstance may be omitted: However I was determined to insert it, though upon no better Authority, because I should be glad to know, supposing the Case to have been exactly as 'tis here related, what could have been done to him?

The Disdain and Confusion of Mind, which naturally rises upon ill Treatment, from those whom we have greatly trusted [12] or loved, might make a Woman in such Circumstances destroy herself. I believe it requires almost as much Fortitude and Resignation as that of a Martyr or Confessor, patiently to acquiesce under such Usage.

If I could hope to find Pardon for the arrogant Thought, I would for once suppose that a Wife might possibly find means to *confine* her Husband in his own House, and to prevent any Attempt for his Releasement, give out that he had crost the Seas, and was in foreign Countries upon his Business or Diversion. Methinks I already hear the Resentment and Indignation of the whole Sex, upon the insolent Supposition! Women were designed for *Domestick Animals*, 'tis but allotting them their proper Place; give them *Needles* and *Prayer Books* there, and there's no great harm done. But to think to confine the *Lords* of the *Creation*, is Insolence beyond a Parallel. It may be so, yet as a Christian, I cannot but think it an excellent Rule to suppose our selves capable of receiving the Treatment we give others, and then to reflect upon the Resentments we should make upon it. *Do unto all Men, as thou wouldest they should do unto thee*, is an universal Precept given to both Sexes, and all Conditions from the Prince upon the [13] Throne, to the Labourer that digs in the Mines.[4]

'Tis true, should a Wife be so audacious as to find Means to confine her Husband, she would be unpardonable; her Guilt would be aggravated by the Relation she stands in to him, by the Respect and Deference she owes him; it would be a kind of *Petty Treason*.[5] But as it is impracticable, I can injure no Man by making the Supposition, which, as a Christian, every Man who has any such Designs upon his Wife, ought to make to himself: Though the Law allows him that Power, Conscience does not. Our very Enemies, as soon as they fall into our Power, though involuntarily, have a Title to our Favour and Protection; all the Laws of Honour and Generosity plead for their gentle Treatment; and shall a Husband be called a Man of Honour, who treats his Wife harshly for no Reason, but because she is in his Power, and which Power he derived from her unbounded Confidence in him? She puts her whole Happiness into his Hands, a Trust for which no Man can give a sufficient Security. She has from hence a Title to his Protection in every Distress: If so, how is a Husband's Guilt aggravated, when he beats, confines, or murders his Wife?

[14] Our Laws decree the more dreadful Death to the guilty Wife, and pronounce a milder Sentence upon the guilty Husband; yet I shall leave it with the Casuists to decide, whether the Breach of *Trust* does not as much aggravate the Sin of Murder in the Husband, as the Breach of *Submission* aggravates the same sin, in the Wife. But whether I am Right in my Sentiments or not, let any Man with the least Christian Charity, Generosity, or common Humanity, consider himself as the Father, Brother or Friend of any of the unfortunate Wives before mentioned; and then say, whether he could not wish, that some Expedient might be found by the Legislature to prevent such Calamities for the Future.

I shall now proceed to consider the Case of Heiresses, there, if any where, the Wife Retains some Property.

The Husband has the Disposal of the whole Income of the Wife's Lands, for his and her Life: And in Cases where the Husband and Wife can join to pass a Fine upon her Lands to raise Money upon any Exigency of their Family, he has Power alone afterwards to mortgage in Consequence of that Fine, and to employ that Money so raised upon his Wife's Estate, according to his particular Pleasure, which perhaps may [15] be upon an Harlot to injure her yet more for her Generosity.

The Laws in being, have provided that no Fine can be levied upon a Wife's Estate, without her full and free Consent openly declared upon that Occasion.[6]

Query, Would it be unreasonable if the same Laws which ordained that no Fine should be levied without her Consent, should determine that her Consent should also be necessary in limiting the Uses of that Fine? The Law in requiring her Consent to the levying the Fine, seems to me to imply that she must be a Judge of the Reasons for which it was levied.

Sometimes a Wife is wise enough to get a Deed executed first, declaring the Uses of the subsequent Fine, which will secure the Money from a Misapplication. But this is no more than a prudential Caution, which is only not contrary to law, but is not required by it, consequently, cannot be called Part of the Law.

By the very Nature of the Marriage Contract, the Husband and Wife acquire a Property in each others Person. Our Laws give the Husband the entire Disposal of the Wife's Person, but she does not seem to retain any Property in his. He may recover Damages of any Man who [16] shall invade his Property in her, but she cannot recover Damages from a Woman, who shall invade her Property in him.[7]

Indeed a Wife may carry her complaint to the spiritual Court, and obtain a Sentence and Costs against the Woman who shall injure her; but 'tis afterwards in the Husband's Power to release these Costs,* which no Doubt any Husband would do, in Favour of a Woman whom he preferred to his Wife. If a Wife impatient of an Injury of this Kind, which is indeed a virtual Dissolution of the Marriage, appeals to the higher Powers for an actual Divorce, 'tis possible she may obtain it, with a small Pittance, with which she may keep herself from Disease and Want. If she brought the whole that the Husband possesses, she may be assigned the fourth or fifth Part, and he (which it must be supposed the Law can give a wise and equitable Reason for) be indulged with the Remainder, to make as just use of, as he had done with the Whole.

[17] I put the Case that the Woman, brought the whole Fortune, because many Men make no Scruple to marry a Woman they don't Love, for the Sake of her

---

*   "If a *Feme Covert* sue another in the spiritual Court, for Incontinency with her Husband, and recover ten Pounds Costs, and the Husband release them, she is by this Barred." *Salkeld*'s Reports of Cases adjudged in the Court of *King's Bench*, Vol.I. p.115. See *Mrs. Hewson*'s Case.

Money; it may therefore be supposed, that Women of Fortune, are more liable to Injuries of that Kind than any other Part of the Sex.

I shall now proceed to consider the Unreasonableness of those Laws, which divest a Woman of all Property in her Children.

As the Law of God gives the Husband the supream Command in his Family, 'tis just that he should have the Disposal of the Children so long as he is in being. But at his Death that Power seems to devolve upon the Wife. She is then the only natural Governor and Guardian of her Children.

I believe there are no Creatures (except of the human Species) where the Male and Female are necessarily concerned in bringing up their joint Offspring; one Parent being sufficient to provide for, and protect them. Nature has not therefore imprest the same instinct on both Sexes, but left the Offspring to the Care of one of them: And amongst those Creatures where neither Parent is necessary, there is no Acknowledgement of the Offspring on either side.

But in the human Species paternal and maternal Care and Affection are found in [18] Nature to be both strong and active; but I believe it will be readily allow'd me that it is in general more so in the Mother. One would therefore suppose that the Mother is in some Degree qualified, as she is more inclined by Nature, to take Care of the Children. In the Levitical Law, we see the Evidence of both Parents necessary, to the Conviction and Punishment of a rebellious Son. We are also told in the sacred Pages that, God has confirmed Authority of the Mother over the Sons. We can't therefore but conclude that God well knew that he had qualified her to give Laws, when he so strictly enjoins the Observation of them.[8]

Since therefore the Light and Instinct of Nature, and the revealed Law of God, both concur in giving Dominion to both Parents, what Authority do we want to plead for that Dominion over our Children, which Nature and the Laws of God give us?

I said before, yet to avoid Misconstruction, I will repeat it again, that the Husband ought to have the Power to dispose of the Children while he lives; but when it has pleased God to provide every Child two Parents, we may suppose one at least, is necessary to him; why then should the Child be deprived of *both in one Day*?

[19] When God, who knows all things perfectly and does all Things wisely, thinks fit to recall one Parent, our Laws give Man, who knows nothing perfectly and does many Things unwisely, the Power to deprive the Child of his other Parent also, by ordering the Child into other Hands, where the Mother's Care and Affection can be of no Service to him.

I confess I never heard of but one Man, who went to the full Extent of his Power in that Instance. He was a Gentleman of a pretty good Estate, and had only one Daughter, to whom he bequeathed his whole Fortune, under this Restriction, that she should forfeit it, if upon any Occasion whatever, she knowingly conversed with, or visited his Widowe after his Death, who was the young Lady's own Mother: And in Case of his Daughter's Disobedience to his Will in this particular, he left his Fortune to an ill-natured Relation of his own, who always hated his Wife, and had been the Occasion of his using her very ill, and who would therefore be sure to take the Advantage of the Forfeiture: The unhappy Mother was therefore constrained to give up all Interest in, and Conversation with her Child for ever; her Jointure being too small to support them both.

[20] I can't figure to myself a more afflictive Circumstance in human Life, than to be entirely deprived of my Child, by the Unkindness of my Husband! When the tenderest, dearest and best founded Affections of the Heart, are baffled, disappointed, and over-ruled, by all-controuling Power, what foreign Accessions of Pleasures or Honours can asswage the Anguish of such a wounded Spirit? Nothing but the most seraphick Love of God, can fill up that vast Vacancy! that most forlorn Void! which an Affectionate well inclined Heart finds in itself, when the tenderest Object of its Love, is ravished from it. 'Tis true, these are rare Instances, but the Law is nevertheless hard, which gives every Husband the Power of exercising such Cruelties.

But in Answer to Remonstrances of this Kind, we are told that the Law supposes the Father the best Judge, whether the Mother is capable of educating their Children.

And also, that it is a Security to the Children, in case the Mother should marry again, and put herself and Children in the Power of another Master.

If we are naturally unqualified to educate our Children, or to chuse proper Persons to assist us in it, then has Nature imprest maternal Affection in vain, at least it ought [21] not to continue any longer than our Children remain in the Nursery, but it should decline and extinguish, as we see it does in other Creatures, when it can be of no further Service to the Offspring.

If we are accidentally disqualified by a foolish trifling Education, where does that Imputation revert, but upon those Persons under whose Direction and Authority we are so educated?

If a second Marriage exposes Children by a Former, to the Oppression of a latter Husband, and utterly disables the Mother to rescue them from it; whence does that Inability arise, but from those Laws which give the Husband so exorbitant a Power over the Wife, that she cannot exert herself in those Duties which God has commanded her to do, unless it be at the Will and Pleasure of her Husband?

The Sum of this Argument is this,

That we are not naturally disqualified to educate our Children, for God gives no natural Instinct in Vain: Not accidentally disqualified, unless by the Fault of the other Sex, in the Education they give us, and the Laws they make for us.

I confess that by the present Laws, we may be deemed disqualified to be intrusted with the Education of our Children, inas- [22] much as the Commands of an Husband, seem to supersede all other Authority whatsoever: At least that appears to be the Sense of the executive Powers, who are supposed to act according to Law; for when the King delegates his executive Authority to his Judges, and a Man and his Wife are brought before them, and indicted for Murder, an horrid Sin against God, and the greatest Sin against the State (except Treason) the Wife as acting under the Command of the Husband shall be acquitted, and the Man hanged. What an Intimation does that give, that our Laws will at least, connive at an Outrage against God, and tearing asunder the very Bands of Society, provided the Woman acts in Obedience to her Husband? That is to be her first Principle, and she is to be judged according to it.

But perhaps it may be said, that in proceeding thus, the Law Regards the Power, not the Authority of the Husband, and that a Wife shall not be acquitted for Murder, unless it appears to have been done in the Presence of the Husband, when the Law supposes some Coercion, which is the Effect of Power, not Authority, his bare Command is nothing.

Whence is that Power supposed to arise? Not from personal Strength, for that would [23] be equally prevalent in all Cases, and a Wife is not exempted from Punishment in Case of Treason, though it should appear that she committed this Treason in Concert with, and in the Presence of her Husband: A supposed Compulsion from personal Strength will not exempt a Boy from Punishment, if he robs, or murders with any Man, except his Father; but the Father's Authority shall excuse the Son, till the Son is at Years of Discretion, when it is supposed that he must understand, that the Command of God supersedes that of a Father, and that it is at his Peril if he does not *obey God rather than Man.*

A Son is not consider'd as a free Agent, when he Acts with his Father, till he comes to the full use of his understanding; and the Indulgence he receives before, is a Favour to the Weakness of his Intellects, not to the Weakness of his Body.

In Short, either Wives can judge how far, and in what Instances an Husband is to be obeyed, or they cannot: If they are so undiscerning as not to be able to perceive the essential Difference between obeying their Husbands in the Lord, and in the direct Opposition to and Defiance of him; then let their blind Obedience to their Husbands excuse them in the Case of Treason as well [24] as it does in other Cases: But if they cannot plead this Darkness of the Understanding, why are they treated like Children or Idiots? I can assign but one Reason for these Inconsistencies, namely, that it is for the Interest of the Community as a Body Politick, that Wives should be punish'd as free Agents for Treason, but that, in Respect to the private Royalties of Husbands, in other Cases they are not expected to judge of Right and of Wrong; 'tis sufficient for them, if their Actions confess they accede to the Jurisdiction of their Husbands.

But if they will still tell us, that this Exemption from Punishment, was designed as a Favour to the Weakness of the Sex, we must take upon our selves to say, that, that Sophistry is vain; we understand better, and know that it is a fine Compliment to the Authority of our domestick Lords and Masters: Had they a real Care for the Sex, they would not grant such an Impunity, which might be a Temptation to commit such Facts, upon which everlasting Damnation is denounced. But they teach us whom to fear. What are their Judgments, if their Mercies are thus Cruel!

That this is their real meaning, give me leave to produce one notable Instance, as it was related in one of the publick Papers some time ago.

[24] A Man and his Wife were found hanged, and their Child murdered in the Cradle in their Bed-chamber, the Door being locked within side, and a Paper lying upon the Table, which Paper contained the Reasons of their laying violent Hands upon themselves and Child, and was subscribed both by the Man's and Woman's Name. The Man was adjudged guilty of Murder and Suicide, and his Body buried in the High-way accordingly; but the Woman being supposed to hang herself at the Command of her Husband, was exempted from further Mischief. Now this was no doubt a considerable Kindness to the Woman, and a great Comfort to the good Husbands in his Majesties Dominions, to provide them a Precedent for commanding their Wives to hang themselves, the Woman being supposed to act upon competent Authority, or the Sentence upon her Body could not have been remitted upon that Consideration. There is a further Reason to deem it an Act of Obedience to Authority, and not a Compliance with Power, since I believe it would be hard to find any Person of so peculiar a Way of thinking, as to be prevailed upon to hang herself for fear of being killed: Unless her Husband had had an Authority as absolute as *Nero*, and sent his Mandate ordering her to dispatch herself in [26] an Hour, or he would have her put to Death with Tortures.

The Woman's Body being permitted to be put in consecrated Ground, was of no real Consequence to her; she was removed from all Interest in this World; her irrecoverable Doom was past, where, I fear, the Command of an Husband would not be deem'd a sufficient Apology for so great a Breach of the Laws of her Creator.* Nor can any think, that was in Truth and Reality the Case; for what worse Consequence could have followed from her resisting her Husband, than her own, and her Child's Death? But it was thought agreeable to our Laws that a Wife should be absolutely at the Command of her Husband, and the Determination was given in Regard to the living, not to the dead.

From hence I must take the Liberty to assert, that this Exemption of a Wife from Punishment, upon Consideration that she obeys her Husband, never was designed as a Privilege to Wives, and that it never can be such in its own Nature, but is a Snare and [27] Temptation to them, to comply with the Command of an Husband be the Instance ever so sinful, and to stand more in awe of a temporary Resentment from him, than of the eternal Resentment of Omnipotence itself.

This is one of the notable Privileges of an *English* Wife. I shall consider a few more of them, as compared to the Privileges of a *Roman* Wife, and see what Figure they make in the Comparison.

---

*   St. *Peter* thought it no Excuse for *Sapphira* that she agreed with her Husband to sin against God; he pronounced the same Sentence upon the Wife, as he had done upon the Husband, which shewed, that he judged their Guilt to be equal. *Acts* Chap.v.

By the Civil Law, Wives have a Right to some Privileges of which the *English* Law wholy divests them. As I apprehend, the Civil or old *Roman* Laws are of no Force, where a Statute, or common Law of *England* contradicts them.

First then,* "The Laws of *Rome* appointed the Wife to be sole Heir, when the Husband dyed without Issue."

The most a Woman can claim by the Laws of *England*, is one third of her deceased Husband's Estate.

Again by the Civil Law,† "a Woman is not constrained to bring her whole Substance as a Portion to her Husband, but may retain back Part of her Goods, [28] which are then called *Paraphernalia*, in which the Husband has no Interest, for she may dispose of them without his Consent, and bring Actions in her own Name for the Recovery of it."

"By the Laws of *England* the *Paraphernalia* are deemed to be only the Woman's wearing Apparel, Ornaments, and Jewels, which adorn her during the Marriage"; which she wears not as hers, and for her own Sake, but as her Husband's, or as it is express'd, suitable to his Quality, and to do him honour.[9] The Presents he makes are bestowed before for that Reason, and they *ipso facto* revert to him as soon as the Solemnity is over.◊ She retains no Property, not even in that sacred Pledge [i.e. her ring], which he had given her as a Token that he would faithfully perform every Article stipulated in the Covenant between them, and which Token, according to the reverend and learned Mr. *Wheatly*, was understood, as⋈ "Livery [29] and Seisin of that Right to his Goods, which she had acquired by becoming his Wife."

Again, though⋈⋈ "by the Civil Law, the Husband during the Marriage, receives the Profits accruing from the Wife's Portion, yet if he declines and grows low in Fortune she may by Law seize her Portion, or Security, or bring her Action against him, and lodge it out of his reach, for the Property of the Portion is not transferred from the Wife by the Intermarriage."

---

* Mr. *Wheatley*'s rational Illustration of the Book of Common Prayer &*c.* p. 439. [Charles Wheatly, *A Rational Illustration of the Book of Common Prayer of the Church of England*, 5th ed. (London, 1728)].

† *Wood*'s New Institute of the Civil Law, p. 53. [The quoted passage most closely matches Thomas Wood, *A New Institute of the Imperial or Civil Law* (London, 1704), 43.]

◊ For although, where *H.* dies interstate, or by Will does not dispose of the Jewels, his Wife may claim (in Case there be no Debts) the Jewels suitable for her Quality, to be worn as Ornaments of her Body, as her *Paraphernalia*; yet it is held in *Crook*'s Reports, that if the Husband by Will devises away the Jewels, such Devise shall stand good against the Wife's Claim of *Paraphernalia Vernon's* Cases argued and adjudged in the High Court of Chancery. Vol. II. p. 246. [*By order of the High Court of Chancery*, vol. 2 (Dublin, [1726]), 246.]

⋈ A rational Illustration of the Book of Common Prayer &*c.* p. 438. [This is loosely paraphrased from Charles Wheatly, *Rational Illustration*; 1728, 1729, p. 438.]

⋈⋈ *Wood*'s New Institute, p. 54. [The comparable passage appears page 44 of the 1704 edition, and page 123 of 1730.]

The Laws of *England* allow a Wife no such Privilege; for if a Man having no real Estate, marries a Woman with any Fortune in Money, and covenants to leave her such a Part of it at his Death, if afterwards she perceives that he designs to spend the whole in his Life-time, she cannot take any Method to prevent it, the Law allowing her no Remedy.

Thus we see that by the Laws of *Rome*, the Wife had her distinct Properties, as well as the Husband. But that by the Laws of *England* she is divested of all Property.

I have been informed by Persons of great Integrity, who have long resided in *Portugal* and consequently had Opportunities of know- [30] ing the Customs of the Country, that a Wife in *Portugal* if she brought never a Farthing, has Power to dispose of half her Husband's Estate by Will; whereas a Woman by our Laws alienates (surrenders, transfers) all her own Property so entirely by Marriage, that if she brought an hundred thousand Pounds in Money, she cannot bequeath one single Penny, even if she left her own nearest and dearest Relations starving for Want.

As there may be some Objections to these Representations, I come now to consider and answer the most material that I can at Present foresee.

Obj. I.[10] As to Mrs. *Lewis*'s Case, there might greater Inconveniencies arise from the Validity of such Wills, than from their Non-Validity. Suppose Mrs. *Lewis* having no Child by her first Husband, had bequeathed her Fortune to a Stranger, and afterwards by her second Husband had had Children, would it not have been hard to have had the Will stand against these Children? However this is a Case that may not happen twice in an Age.

My Design in these Representations, is to shew the Scope and Tendency of the *English* Laws in Relation to Wives, and that they sink us lower than Captivity itself, [31] of which this Case is one notorious Instance. As for any Advantage which might arise to Children, from the Invalidity of such Wills, from some particular unforeseen Contingency; that by no Means destroys my Assertion. The Wit of Man cannot contrive a Law of such universal Influence, as to reach every particular Case that may happen. If therefore we should find some Exempt Case, in which some particular Woman might be favoured by those very Laws which oppress Wives in General, it would only shew that Man, cannot controul Events, and that God can, and does, bring Good out of Evil. But after all, it cannot be suppos'd that Mrs. *Lewis*, or any Woman in her Senses, would suffer a Will to remain in Force to the Prejudice of her own Children; and that such Wills should remain uncancelled by Accident, or Forgetfulness, or the like, could never be foreseen by the Makers of this Law; neither can it be us'd as an Argument for the Justification of it. The Reason of this Law is easily seen, the Consequences of it, as to particular Cases are and must be unforeseen, as well as the Number of Persons who should be declared in a worse Condition than that of Captivity itself, by it.

[32] *Obj.* II. By the Laws of *England*, a Woman who has been beat and abus'd by her Husband, may swear the Peace against him, and if he can't find Security for his Behaviour, send him to Jail.

To which I answer, *First*, that sometimes this Relief cannot be had, the Husband having it in his Power to lock up his Wife, and so prevent her Complaint, as in some Cases already cited.

Secondly, That the Consequences of this Relief, (if it may be so called) bring great Hardships upon the Wife.

1.   As it exposes her to the Resentment of her Husband at his Return Home, without abating his Power, which is so great, that he may revenge himself a thousand Ways not cognizable by the Law.

2.   That if he is a Tradesman, or a Labourer, she, and her Family depend upon him for Bread, and the Consequence of his lying in Jail must be, that she, and her Family must starve.

Obj. III. The Wife may put her Fortune into Trustees Hands before Marriage, and by that Means secure it for her own Use.

I acknowledge this to be available, if done [33] with the Consent of her intended Husband, otherwise the Court of Chancery will relieve him. But if we reflect how extremely ignorant all young Women are as to points in Law, and how their Education and Way of Life, shuts them out from the Knowledge of their true Interest in almost all things, we shall find that their Trust and Confidence in the Man they love, and Inability to make use of the proper Means to guard against his Falsehood, leave few in a Condition to make use of that Precaution. And it is too notoriously known, that it has seldom been of Service to those who have done it, the Husband having so entirely the Disposal of the Wife's Person, that he easily finds Means to bend her to his Will, insomuch that I have heard, that it is a frequent saying of one of our present eminent Judges, "that he had hardly known an Instance, where the Wife had not been kissed or kicked out of any such previous Settlement."

Obj. IV. A Wife cannot be said to be divested of all Property, since she does retain a reversionary Property in her Jointure, which is out of the Husband's Power to alienate.

[34] To which I reply, that supposing she does retain that reversionary Property (which considering the Authority of the Husband she may not always be able to do) yet Jointures are not sufficient for all Occasions.

Few Wives who have Jointures, have any other Provision, and all Wives who have no other Provision, may be liable to the Hardships which I shall exemplify in the following Case.

A young Lady, well born, with five thousand Pounds to her Portion, married a Gentleman possest of an hundred and seventy Pounds *per Annum*, which she accepted of, as a Jointure for her five thousand Pounds. As the Gentleman was one of the learned Professions, he had besides his real Estate, some Places which brought him in a considerable Revenue: Before this Marriage he was bound for his Father, for a large Sum of Money, and was also in Debt himself; both which he concealed from her, neither did she ever know it, till after his Death, which happened five Years after their Marriage. In that Time she had had four Children, and was breeding of the fifth when he died. Her Father-in-law died a Month before her Husband, and in a short Time after her Husband's Death the old Gentleman's principal Creditor took out Letters of Admini- [35] stration, by Virtue of which he seized her Husband's personal Estate to answer the Money for which he was bound for his Father. But the personal Estate not amounting to that Money, the Administrator shewed no Mercy to the unhappy Widow, but took even her Wedding Ring, from her Finger, and all moveables, except the Cloaths on her own, and her Children's Backs at the Time of the Seizure. The Widow was then left with Four Children, a naked House, and an hundred and seventy Pounds per *Annum* Jointure. She became a Widow within a few Days after an half yearly Payment from the Tenant, who rented this Estate; consequently she could make no Demand upon him for near half a Year after. Within which Time, she was to support the Expenses of her Lying-in as well as to provide for the four Children she had already.

As these, or the like Circumstances may happen to any Woman who has only a Jointure to depend upon, I would therefore recommend it to the unmarried of my Sex, to secure by Article such a Sum of Money as will support them during such an Exigency, till their Jointures shall come in. I confess 'tis very rare that we see a Woman stript so bare, as this Lady, whose Case I last re-[36] lated, which still strengthens my Assertion, that the Law in this Instance is hard, since it shews it to be against the general Sense and Humanity of Mankind to go to the Extent of it.

Obj. V. The Laws obliging men to pay their Wives Debts contracted before Marriage is as hard upon them.

I believe not; Womens Debts being more easily known than Mens, they having many Ways of concealing and misrepresenting their Circumstances which Women have not.

All Men in Trade have their Affairs so complicated, that it is an hard matter to find out what their Debts are.

A Man may by the treacherous Kindness of a Friend be put in Possession of a Fortune in Order to obtain a Woman with Money, and secretly contract to pay it all back again as soon as he is married. That is, as soon as he has got her Money, that being all which he considered.

A Spend-thrift may buy a young Heiress of those about her, and afterwards pay the purchase money out of her Estate.

Obj. VI. These are Tricks and Cheats, which the Law neither ordains, nor is answerable for.

[37] I acknowledge they are Tricks* and Cheats, and no Part of the Law itself; yet they are practicable in Consequence of the Law, which gives the sole Property of the Wife's Fortune to the Husband, by which he is enabled to pay the Debts contracted to purchase her, out of her own Estate. 'Tis true, a Woman may impose upon a Man, by telling him she has a Fortune when she has none, and (if the Man is weak enough) by Artifice engage him to marry her upon that Supposition. But she can't borrow a Sum of Money, and at her Marriage put her Husband in Possession of it as her Fortune, and afterwards secretly repay it, out of his Substance without his Knowledge: And if the Husband should be called upon to repay the Money, he would require to know the Consideration upon which it was lent, by which Means it might appear that the Creditor had combined with his Wife to impose upon him, and cheat him; and in that Case the Law would relieve him.

I shall produce an Instance of Fraud, by Way of Illustration.

A Farmer's Son courted a young Woman with whom he was extreamly in Love; [38] but as she had no Fortune, the Father of the young Man refused his Consent to the Marriage, unless some of her Friends would give her an hundred Pounds. The Lover made this Report to an Aunt of the young Woman's, with whom she then lived. The Aunt gave her Niece an hundred Pounds, but at the same time took a Bond of the Lover for so much Money lent to him, which he was to repay at the Time specified in the Bond. Upon this they were married with the Father's Consent, who gave his Son a considerable Part of his Substance. Afterwards upon the Non-payment of this hundred Pounds, the Aunt applied herself to her Council to know in what Manner she could proceed to recover the Money. But she was informed, that the Money was not to be recovered; it being a Cheat upon the old Man, therefore none of his Substance, which he had given his Son in Consideration of that hundred Pound, should satisfy that Debt. As the young Man would not voluntarily repay it, she was advised to be contented with the Loss of what she could not recover. I don't produce this as an adjudged Case, for it never was tryed, the Aunt being informed by Men of great Reputation for their Abilities [39] in the Law, that the Money was irrecoverable.

If the Husband is not obliged to repay the Money for which he had given his own Bond, because another Person would be cheated by it, much less shall he be obliged to repay that Money, which his Wife borrowed before Marriage in Order to cheat him.

As there are more Instances in which Men can impose upon Women, in the Representation of their Circumstances before Marriage, than there are in which Women can impose upon Men; so Men can secretly pay their Debts, after Marriage, which Women cannot; which must necessarily make them more cautious how they

---

* Does the Law make any Provision against these Tricks and Cheats? If it does not, is not the Law so far defective?

conceal or misrepresent their Circumstances, since that must expose them to the Resentment of an injured Husband, who, as he has the Power of, would seldom want the Inclination to Revenge.

Whosoever makes any Observations of this Kind, will (I believe) find in Fact, that Men suffer very little from being answerable for their Wives Debts contracted before Marriage, in Comparison to what Women suffer, from their Fortunes being liable to pay their Husbands Debts contracted before Marriage.

[40] *Obj.* VI. [sic] Amends is made for all this by Womens Exemption from Imprisonment in Civil Causes.

'Tis fit indeed they should be exempted, as having no Property, and consequently no Way of getting out again; but this Exemption was never intended as a Favour to them; however it may sometimes accidentally become so.

One Reason of such Exemption I take to be this, that a Woman's lying in Jail will pay no Man his Money, and so some Persons might chance to become Losers by her; 'tis therefore Decreed, that her Husband who possesses her Property, shall be answerable for her Debts.

The Civil Law assigns another Reason for the Exemption of Wives from a Jail in Civil Causes, namely, that there is too great an Hazard of having their Chastity attempted in such Confinement.

I suppose our *English* Husbands are more tenacious of their Property in that Point than the *Romans* were, and would be more uneasie at the Invasion of it: Not that they consider the Woman in an higher Character, as a Christian, and for her own sake, to keep her out of the Temptation, and sinning against the Law of God; for if that [41] were any Part of their Consideration, it is to be supposed, that they would be as tender of their own Souls; and to deter an Husband from Unfaithfulness to his Wife, and all others from joining in his Sin against her, would empower her to expose him, by sueing the Woman, and recovering Damages of her, for invading her Right, in the same Manner as the Law empowers the Husband to recover Damages for the like Offence. For the Transgression against God, is as great in the Husband, as in the Wife, and equally damnable in both: Tho' there is one Circumstance, which renders it a greater Injury to the Man in his civil Capacity.

Obj. VII. Whether the Exemption of Wives from a Jail in Civil Causes, was originally designed as a Favour to them, is not the Question; if that Exemption is a Recompence for divesting them of all Property, the Law is justified, whatever Motive it proceeded upon in decreeing such Exemption.

I reply then, full to the Question, That it is not a Recompence.

To divest a Man of all Property, and then exempt him from a Jail in Consequence of his Debts, is just such a Privilege in his [42] Civil Capacity, as it would be in his Natural one, to divest him of all Pleasure, and in Return to decree that he should feel no Pain. As such Exemption from Pleasure and Pain would, in Effect, strike him out of *Being* as a *Man*, so such divesting him of all Property, with such Exemption from Payment of *Debts*, is, in Effect, to cut him off from being a Member of *Civil* Society.

As a Man would chuse to retain his Natural Pleasures, and run the Hazard of Natural Pains, so he would chuse to retain his Civil Rights, and run the Hazard of Civil Inconveniencies.

Till it shall appear that these are not parallel Cases, I believe I may conclude, that *Exemption* from *Debts* is not a Recompence for divesting of Property.

Obj. VIII. But still the Distinction as to the *Roman* Captives remains un-answered, namely, that Marriage is a voluntary Act,* and that Women are not forced into it.

I suppose it cannot be said, to be always voluntary, for in many Instances Women [43] are commanded and directed into it, by their Parents and Guardians, and in some other Circumstances 'tis their only Way of advancing themselves, and settling in the World.

Indeed as to many Persons, 'tis their own free Choice, to whom Marriage with its complicated Hazards, appears more eligible than the solitary, unfriend'd, ridiculed Condition of a single Life; and no wonder, since the usual Way of edu-cating young Women seems as if it were calculated on Purpose to awaken all the Affections of the Heart, at the same Time that it deprives them of their proper Counter-balance, the Strength of the Head.

That which glitters in the Eye, strikes the Fancy, and charms the Imagination, being represented to them, as the most improving Objects for their Contemplation and Learning. The Attainment of a fine Air, a graceful Motion, an elegant Fancy in Dress, a Knowledge of the fashionable Compliments and Civilities, at receiv-ing and paying Visits, with more Accomplishments of the like Importance, are recommended to them, as the surest Means of obtaining the Love and Admiration of the Men, and procuring an advantageous Settlement in Marriage, which is proposed to them, [44] as their highest Advancement, and End and Design of all their Attainments.

Can any one suppose that a young Creature thus disciplined, should ever take it into her Head, that her truest Happiness, as well as greatest Honour, should arise from the Service of God, and free Exertion of her own Soul? That she should Endeavour by all Means to attain a Fund of Reason, Learning, and Knowledge sufficient to furnish Entertainment for her whole Life?

---

*   Does this voluntary Act, tend to the Good of the Community? If it does, is not its being voluntary a Merit? Should it not therefore entitle us to Privilege and Favour. If involuntary, and we suffer from it; to Pity and Relief, as far as it can be given?

Thus having no Notion of true Worth in herself, she is as little a Judge of it in others, but resigns herself to the Ignorant, the Vain, or the Vicious, as they come recommended by Title, Equipage, or Fortune.

I would not from hence be thought to infer, that none but foolish Women marry, or that Celibacy is preferable to Marriage, with a Man of Worth. I would only give some Check to that Triumph, and Self-admiration which some Men are apt to conceive, upon an Observation, that most Women are willing to marry at some time or other; by shewing that they are disqualified from the very beginning for the true Enjoyment of their own Minds, and therefore [45] notwithstanding all Disadvantages, are willing to admit of a foreign Assistance.

Since their Choice is in a great Measure determined by their Education, and their Education is at the Discretion of the Men, I would use this as an Argument why they should find some Redress for their great Calamities, when they happen to meet with a Tyrant and Oppressor, where they had hoped to have found an indulgent Friend, and faithful Guardian.

As Marriage is the very Basis, Foundation, and Cement of Society, an Institution of God, and productive of the greatest Blessings in human Life, 'tis highly reasonable to guard it with such Laws, that those who turn it into a Plague and a Curse, might receive due Punishment for such enormous Transgressions!

If there are any Laws which empower a Woman to ruin or oppress her Husband, you have the Power in your own Hands; in God's Name let them be amended.

Obj. IX. Notwithstanding all this, *England* is the Paradise of Women, they are better treated here than in any other Part of the World.

But it may be answered, that *England* is also, the Paradise of Men, no Subjects [46] enjoying such invaluable Privileges as they do here: And it would be thought a very unjust Reply from an arbitrary Prince in Defence of his tyrannical Proceedings, that he treated his Subjects better here, than the Grand Seignior treated his Slaves in *Turkey*.

Obj. X. All these are rare Cases, and for the generality Wives have no Reason to complain.

But no Thanks to the Laws of our Country for that Exemption; let every particular Woman who is well treated, thank God and her Husband for the Blessing. At the same Time, she may reflect, that she is in the Condition of a Slave, tho' she is not treated as such, according to the Opinion of a late eminent Member of the House of Commons, who declared in that honourable Assembly, that he thought "that Nation in a State of Slavery, where any Man had it in his Power to make them so, tho' perhaps the Rod might not always be held over their Backs."

Tho' I have taken the Liberty to speak my sense of these Laws, and the Consequences of them, which are the Causes of our Complaint; and also to answer some Objections, which I suppos'd might be made, [47] yet I don't presume to address my self to the Legislature to argue, but to refer it to them to decide, and shall humbly and readily acquiesce to their Determinations, upon this and all other Occasions.

But till I am better informed, I hope I may be pardoned, if I confess that I hardly believe it possible to reconcile these Laws, with the Rights and Privileges of a free People. That there should be so great a Part of the Community, who have never been notorious Offenders against it, entirely deprived of their Liberty, or even of making Use of their Ingenuity and Industry to procure them a Subsistance, when those who should provide it for them, refuse it, or are incapable of it.

I suppose the prime Design, and ultimate End of all equitable Governments, is so to proportion Authority and Subjection, that they may in some sort Counterpoise each other; by investing the *Governing* with such *Prerogatives*, and allowing the *Governed* such *Privileges*, that each Part may be provided for, according to their several just Pretensions; and that no one Set of People might be exposed to Oppression, either from their publick or private Governors; that Order and Equity may run through all Ranks, and compose one uniform collective Body.

[48] 'Tis from these Considerations (I apprehend) that our Laws forbid the buying and selling Men, there being such an absolute Inconsistency in the Conditions of a Freeborn *English* Man and a Slave, that they will by no Means comport in the same Community.

From hence also, one Part of domestick Authority is relaxed from what it was amongst the *Romans*. With them a Son was esteemed so much at the Father's Disposition, that by an obsolete Law, the Father was invested with the Power of Life and Death; but afterwards with that of moderate Correction only; yet the Son was still his Father's Property, and could be freed from his Jurisdiction only by being advanced to some dignified Office in the State, or by Emancipation.

The Father's Power over the Son's Property also was very correspondent to that over his Person: But this domestick Authority, being thought inconsistent with the Nature of our free Constitution, which admits not of arbitrary Proceedings, at the Age that a Child is supposed to be able to judge for himself, he is at his own Disposal, as is also his Property.

What I would observe from hence is, that tho' domestick Authority is lessened as to [49] Children, that it is augmented as to Wives, as I have shewn in the foregoing Instances, and that Wives have not a Degree of Liberty and Property, correspondent to that Degree of Liberty and Property, which is allowed all other subordinate Persons in the whole Community.

Omnipotence itself disclaims the Power of doing Evil, the exact Rectitude of the Will of the Almighty is an everlasting Restriction.

Our King, his happiest and greatest Viceregent upon Earth, lays no Claim to the Power of Oppression: and it is no more to the Diminution of his Honour, than it is to the Restraint of his Actions, that our Laws guard us from suffering by his Authority.

Since then, the God of Heaven and Earth, in and from himself, acts always by the Rules of Justice and Mercy; and our Sovereign knows it to be his most distinguishing Honour to be under Obligations to govern his People, by the same unerring Rules; shall I be accused of Confidence or Presumption, for humbly beseeching that our domestick Lords, may be under the same happy Obligations in their private Capacities, which are so true an Honour to our King, in his most illustrious Station?

I hope the Justice and Integrity of my own [50] Heart which acquits me before God, will also plead my Excuse before Men, for making these Representations; especially since I apprehend, that I am justified by the Laws of the Land, which allow every *English* Subject, the Privilege to speak his own Grievances.

It is reported of a magical Ring of *Gyges*'s, that it had an extraordinary Power of making the Wearer of it invisible. A Person being asked, what a Man of Honour would do had he such a Ring? He was answered, just the same as he would without it. All Men who have the least Notion of Honour, would readily acquiesce in the Justness of this Reply: But I believe few who know the present Disposition of the World, would think it very politick to present every Man in his Majesty's Dominions with such a Ring; lest the Power of doing Mischief, might create, as well as assist an Inclination to it.

A Man of Honour would not desire such a Ring; a Man without Honour should not be trusted with it.

A good Husband would not desire the Power of Horse-whipping, confining, Half-starving his Wife, or squandering her Estate; a bad Husband should not be allowed it.

A good Husband would never feel the Restraint; a bad one, would ultimately find the [51] Advantage of it; inasmuch as he has a Master to whom he must render an Account of the Use of his delegated Authority.

But if after all, these Representations should not be thought worthy the Consideration of the Legislature, or if they should be considered, and we should yet fail of obtaining any Relief; either because the Legislature cannot find proper Means, or wants the Inclination to give it; there is still one Part of my Sex, who may receive some Advantage from them; namely, the Unmarried, to whom I now Address myself, entreating them to consider the Hazards they run, when they venture an Alliance with the other Sex, who were designed by Nature for their *Counter-parts*, but who have taken upon themselves to be the *whole*, insomuch that they have voted us *Dead in Law*, except in criminal Causes. They do us indeed the Favour to consider us as real Persons, when they think fit to *burn* or *hang* us: This is *incorporating* with a Vengeance! *They swallowed us up quick, when they were so wrathfully displeased at us!*[11]

But God be thanked, I have an Husband who lets me be *alive*, and gives me leave to be *some Body*, and to tell other People what I think they are.

[52] I am persuaded there are many Wives in *England*, who by the Favour of their Husbands, are still in a State of *Existence:* And am also sensible, that some Wives have so little Apprehension of this Law of *Annihilation*, that they are in Fact the *freer* Agents of the two. But at Present I am not enquiring into Facts, I am reporting what I take to be the Law, in Order to have the Hardships of it known at least, that if they can't be amended, they may be avoided, by making Women more cautious, how they deliver themselves into the Hands of a Man, *lest he bring them to nothing.*[12]

At the same Time that I warn my own Sex, I must do Justice to the other; and acknowledge, that I believe there are very many of them, to whom human Laws, as to their domestick Behaviour, are entirely superfluous:

Who bear their Faculty so meek, have been
So clear in their great Office, that their Virtues
Will plead like Angels.   Macbeth.[13]

There is no Character in private Life, so venerable and amiable, as that of a good Husband. The accumulated Praises which are due, to the tender affectionate *Lover*, the endearing generous *Friend*, the discreet *Guide*, and faithful *Guardian*, are his, in [53] the most eminent Degree; with this peculiar Addition, that the Impunity with which he *might* Sin against his Wife, is with him the strongest Reason why he never *will* do it.

Tho' there are *Good* Husbands yet have a Care of *Bad*: With this last piece of Advice I shall leave the unmarried Women.

I come now to consider one Objection, which still remains against all I can say, and which I am sensible no Art or Eloquence, can ever obviate, namely, *my Sex*. Custom and Education has dwindled us into very Trifles! such meer Insignificants! that it may be thought Presumption and Folly in one of us, to presume to plead our own Cause, even tho' it should appear to be upon the most justifiable Pretensions.

Notwithstanding this discouraging Reflection, I shall

First, Proceed to the Sentiments of two speculative Authors, who have considered human Nature abstracted from all external Laws, and see in what Light they place us.

Secondly, I shall refer my self to the Judgment of a most judicious Reasoner upon Revelation.

Thirdly, I shall make some Observations [54] upon the Quotations from these Authors, and draw some Conclusions which I think follow from their Principles.

Fourthly, I shall explain the original Curse of Subjection passed upon the Woman, and shew that the Laws of *England* go far beyond it.

First, Mr. *Wollaston* in his Religion of Nature represents the two Sexes, as exact Counter Parts to each other, he speaks,* "of the Interchange of Affections, and a Conspiration of all their Counsels and Measures, the Qualities and Abilities of the one Sex being fitted, and as it were tallying to the Wants of the other. Many things there are which may be useful, perhaps necessary to the Man, and yet require the delicater Hand and nicer Management and Genius of the Woman: And so the Woman, cannot but want many things which require the more robust and active Powers, or greater Capacity of the Man."

Again, "† I have designedly forborn to mention that Authority of an Husband over his Wife, which is usually given [55] to him, not only by private Writers, but even by Laws, because I think it has been carried much *too high*. I would have them live so far upon the *Level*, as (according to my constant Lesson) to be governed both by Reason. If the Man's Reason be *Stronger*, or his Knowledge and Experience *greater* (as 'tis commonly supposed to be) the Woman will be obliged upon that Score to pay a Deference and *submit* to him."

It seems to me from hence, that Mr. *Wollaston*, founds all Authority in the wedded State upon a *Superiority of Reason*; therefore let that Superiority happen on either Side, the same Consequence must follow from it, and no Doubt, as the World now is, it would generally fall to the Men; they having the Advantages of Universities, publick Negotiations, and a free unconstrained Converse with Mankind, in Pursuance of their several Professions, Arts, and Occupations.

But if we argue from a State of Nature, we must consider the Abilities of each Sex, antecedently to these accidental Advantages; and we do not see in Fact, that, amongst the vulgar unlearned People, Men are so much *wiser* than Women, as to induce us to suppose that their natural Endowments are much greater.

[56] Yet as we never were, or can be in a State of Nature, I don't presume to contend for an Equality, but acknowledge that God has for very wise Reasons invested Man with the Superiority; but without Recourse to Revelation, I believe it would be a hard Task to justify the carrying the Authority of the Husband, higher than Mr. *Wollaston* has done.

But I will for once, even with Mr. *Hobbs* [sic], suppose we were in a State of Nature, and see what he says would be the Consequence of it.

"◊ And thus in a State of Nature, every Woman that bears Children becomes at once both a Mother and a Lord. But what some say that in this Case, the Father by Reason of the Pre-eminence of Sex, and not the Mother, becomes Lord,

---

*   *Religion of Nature, &c.* p.155.
†   *Religion of Nature*, 159.
◊   Philosophical Rudiments concerning Government and Society, Chap. ix. p.136. [*Philosophical Rudiments concerning Government and Society* (1651), the English translation of Thomas Hobbes's *De Cive* (1642)]

signifies nothing. For both Reason shews the contrary, because the Inequality of their natural Forces is not so great, as that the Man could get the Dominion without War; and Custom also contradicts not, for Women, namely *Amazons*, have in former Times waged War with their Adversaries, and disposed of their Children [57] according to their Wills: And at this Day in divers Places Women are vested with the principal Authority, neither do their Husbands dispose of their Children but themselves; which in Truth they do by the Right of Nature, forasmuch as they who have the supreme Power are not tied at all (as has been shewed) to the Civil Law. Add also, that in a State of Nature it cannot be known who is the Father, but by the Testimony of the Mother; the Child therefore is his, whose the Mother will have it, and therefore hers; wherefore original Dominion over Children belongs to the Mother."

And this Author allows of no other original Dominion.

I have a great Abhorrence of the whole Scope and Design of this Author in his Writings, and think it not only wicked but absurd to write to us as in a State of Nature, when we can prove from better Authorities than his, that we never were in a State of Nature, or can be so, so long as we have a Possibility of consulting the Bible. Yet supposing we were in a State of Nature, this, and many other things which he says, are (I believe) incontestably true.

Secondly, There is a very learned and ingenious Author, with whom I am so happy [58] as to correspond in my Opinion concerning the Equality of the Sexes at their first Creation, and also their Inequality upon the Transgression. I must therefore take the Liberty to quote his Sentiments, tho' I heartily beg his Pardon for introducing him in such Company as Mr. *Hobbs*, and acknowledge that I think neither he, nor even the celebrated Mr. *Wollaston*, worthy to be named with him, much less in Contradiction to him.

"* And that this Subjection in the Woman is the Effect of a Curse, consequent to that Offence which wrought our Fall, is evident, because on Supposition that human Nature were in a State of Perfection, where Reason ruled and Perverseness had no Place, there seems to be no imaginable Reason why one Sex should be in Subjection to the other: And accordingly we find, that the Woman was given at first under no other Character but that of a Companion, because it was *not good for Man to be alone*; nor did *Adam* consider her under any other Character, for when he excuses his Offence to almighty [59] God, by charging it upon his Compliance with *Eve*, he says,† *the Woman whom thou gavest to be with me, she gave me of the Tree, and I did eat. The Woman whom thou gavest to be with me,* i.e. whom thou gavest to be my Associate and Companion, without the least hint of Subjection, and Dependency. Nor was there the least Reason for any in that State, as I shewed before."

*   Revelation examined, &c. Vol. I. p.110.
†   *Gen.* iii. 12.

We see it is the Opinion of this Orthodox Divine, that the Sexes were equal before the Fall: And that after the nicest Search Mr. *Wollaston* and Mr. *Hobbs* could make into Nature, they could find no Foundation in Nature for that very great Superiority which is ascribed to the Man.

How comes it to pass then, that the Opinions and Customs of all Nations should give him that Superiority, even where 'tis supposed they could have had no Information of the Curse of Subjection passed upon the Woman? I say all Nations, the Exceptions being too few to destroy a general Rule, tho' enough to establish Mr. *Hobbs*'s Assertion, that the Superiority is not founded in Nature.

[60] In answer to the foregoing Question, I reply that all Nations are the Progeny of *Adam* and *Eve*, and that for some Ages after their Children branched out into Families, they must have had a Tradition of the Curse of Subjection passed upon the Woman, and formed the Government of their Families accordingly: When Men became more numerous upon the Earth, and united themselves into greater Communities, that Authority was kept up, even where 'tis possible the Tradition might be lost upon which it was first founded. And when Men had the Authority, tho' they might not all know that it was by divine Appointment, it is not to be imagined that they would voluntarily give it up, but would rather transmit it from Generation to Generation. And thus it must be from the very Words of the Curse, which not only implied a Command to the Wife to obey her Husband, but constrained also a positive Declaration that she should be in that Subjection, to which God then commanded her Acquiescence.

It is somewhat beside my present Purpose, yet I would observe here, that as this universal Subjection of the Sex must arise from this Origin, it is one good Evidence of the Truth of Revelation, for since it is not a Law of Nature, how should such a Custom [61] spread itself through all Nations in all Ages, if it did not take its Rise from Revelation at first.

If this is not allowed to be an Argument for the Truth of Revelation, let any Man assign some other Cause for this universal Subjection of the Sex; and if it appears to be a true one, I shall readily acquiesce in it; and the rather, because I can bring no Authority for thus applying this Argument.

Thirdly, I come now to explain and account for the Curse of Subjection passed upon the Woman, and to shew that the Laws of *England* go far beyond it.

I plead for no female Usurpation, nor am for disannulling the Laws of the Almighty, which are founded upon eternal Justice, Mercy and Wisdom. I willingly and humbly acquiesce to the Sentence of the Judge of all the Earth, *"Since thou hast done this, thy Desire shall be unto thy Husband, he shall rule over thee."* Yet tho' I submit to the Executors of divine Vengeance, I would not be ruled by a *Rod of Iron*, nor corrected *by Scorpions*.[14]

"Wherewithal a Man sins, therewith shall he be punished."[15] Wherewithal God punishes, therewith doth he save. His [62] Mercy is as conspicuous as his Justice,

and engages our Love and Praise to the gracious Father, and our Adoration and Reverence to the awful Judge!

Behold this Curse in its true Light, and it will appear in its End and Design to have been a Blessing.

The very Essence of Sin is Disobedience, and the first Person who disobeyed God upon Earth, was the Woman: Since therefore she would not submit to the Law of her Creator, she was put in Subjection to her Equal.

The Christian Religion as a Consequence of *Christ*'s Coming, was foretold at the Time of the Curse: Which as it is a self-denying Scheme, so that Condition which has the most frequent Opportunities of practicing Self-denial in its ordinary Occurrences, will be ultimately the most advantageous. The most indifferent Action which a Woman does at the Command of her Husband, from a Sense that God has commanded her to obey him, becomes an Act of Religion, and as such, is rewardable to all Eternity. 'Tis frequently a complicated Act of Virtue; 'tis always Obedience, which includes Humility; and 'tis many Times self denial, and a Conquest over her own Passions.

[63] Thus far I have spoken of the Justice and Mercy of God's Sentence, give me Leave now to consider the Wisdom of it.

Moral Virtues are in their very Nature the Objects of our Understandings; they are so many divine Truths, which whoever perceives cannot but perceive their Excellence; but yet this Perception of Truth or the bare Knowledge of our Duty is not sufficient to make us act agreeable to it: The *Will* whose Province it is to *obey* and execute the Dictates of *Reason*, is continually rebelling against and usurping Authority over it; it not only stops us in the Pursuit of Truth, makes us wink hard and shut our Eyes against the Light, but even where it cannot thus hood-wink our Understanding, it frequently exerts its Tyranny the more, and makes us act in Contradiction to it. It is this Malignity in the Will of Man that occasions all the Evils and Disorders of the moral World; somewhat therefore besides the bare Excellence of Virtue was greatly wanting to correct and abate its Virulence; and to this End are directed God's *Positive Commands*. The Beauty and Excellence of Virtue influenced even our first Parents no longer than while they obeyed God's positive Command, and had no irregular Passions, Prejudices, or evil Ha- [64] bits, to hinder their Perception of, and compliance with Truth. And to us, who lie under the unhappy Byass of a Nature depraved by original Sin, and the Dominion of so many vagrant Affections, which continually cloud the Understanding and stir up the Will to rebel, positive Commands were *absolutely necessary*, even to put us in a Condition of perceiving and practicing moral Virtues, by bending and subduing the Will, rectifying and weakening the Affections and Appetites, that they might be less able to pervert, and impose upon the Under-standing.

I believe it would be easie to shew, that this has always been God's Method of Proceeding, by applying to the Will according as he saw Occasion. The *Jews* being a Stiff-necked, perverse People, and almost all *Will*, had their religious Worship encompassed, and fenced round with outward Observances, many of which there appears no Reason to have kept, but as they were the direct Command of their divine Legislator. As *Christ*'s Coming was foretold at the Time of the Curse, and he being designed to root out, and destroy the whole Body of Sin; and the Seat of Sin being in the Will, it was necessary under his Dispensation also, that there should be Laws which bore par- [65] ticular Respect to the *Will*, in order to enforce its Concurrence with the Understanding in our bounden Duty and Service. "*His Servants ye are, whom ye yield your selves to obey.*"[16]

The Understanding recognises God's Title, but the Will secures his Possessions.

Upon this View, I believe it will appear agreeable to God's Wisdom that, That Sex which gave the first Proof of a disobedient Will, should have an additional Restraint upon it, to disappoint and over-rule it, that for the Future it might be less able to contend with the Understanding, and the Law of God.

It is still a farther Testimony of God's Wisdom to invest Man with this restraining Authority, the more frequently to remind even him, of God's Indignation against those who should presume to disobey his *positive Commands*, by making him the Executor of his Resentment upon it: Who tho' a Delinquent himself, yet his Sin admitted of greater Alleviations than the Woman's, and consequently had a milder Punishment: And her Punishment great as it was, if humbly submitted to, would naturally produce the most lasting Blessings.

If then it is agreeable to Justice, Mercy and Wisdom, it is established upon such [66] Foundations that it is our true Interest that our Obligations to obey our Husbands should remain, *till the Fashion of this World passeth away*; then will be accomplished our most blooming Hopes and animating Expectations, the Laws of Equality will then forever be set Right, and, *she that humbleth herself, shall be exalted!*[17]

But tho' God thus punishes his Servants in Mercy, yet he never condemned them to be *put under Axes, and Harrows of Iron, nor to pass through the Brick-kiln!*[18] These were Punishments for the Heathen, *which called not upon his Name.* 'Tis therefore no Excuse for us, that the Women in *Turkey* are used worse than we are. We abhor a Comparison with them, as much as the Men would here, a Comparison of their Condition with that of their Sex in Turkey.

When the Men refuse to bear their Part of the Curse, with what Equity can they require us, to bear ours? *In the sweat of thy Brows shalt thou eat Bread.*[19] But when they refuse to stir a Finger for their Support, is it equitable that they should tye their Wives Hands behind them, and make their helpless Offspring Fatherless and Motherless also?

"*My Ways are equal, O! House of Israel, your Ways are unequal. What have I required of thee, O Man! but to do Justice, to* [67] *love Mercy, and to walk humbly with thy God?* "[20]

As the Woman's Sin was in the undue Gratification of her *Will*, in her *Will* shall she be punished: She shall depend upon her Husband in all Matters of Pleasure, Diversion, and Delight: Her *Desires* should be circumscribed by his, whom she should reverence in Acquiescence to divine Authority: He should have the supreme Command in his Family, and she should act in Subordination to him.

This I humbly apprehend to be the Scripture Extent and Meaning of the Curse. And not that God precluded himself from any farther Authority over the Woman; by delivering her so far into the Power of her Husband, as that she might rob and murder at his Command.

Neither did he preclude the Woman from doing any Good, except she had her Husband's Command or Permission.

He orders all Parents to provide for their Children according to their Abilities.

But our Laws give an Husband the Power to supersede that Command, by allowing him to take all things from his Wife, and then to prevent her obtaining any thing more, by her Labour or Ingenuity. Her intellectual and personal Abilities seem to be her [68] own, since no Pacts can transfer them to another, yet her Husband can prevent her Exertion of them, either for herself or Children, even when he won't do any thing for them himself.

Again, God commands all Parents to *breed up their Children in the Nurture and Admonition of the Lord.*[21]

But an Husband may prevent his Wife's doing that Duty, even after his Death, when they have no Parent but a Mother, by ordering the Children into other Hands, tho' no other can be so nearly concern'd for them.

I beg to know whether we have not a Right by Nature, to be permitted to do all that Good, which God has given us Abilities to do?

And whether it can be supposed that God gave Man an Authority in Opposition to his own?

And whether by the Nature of Societies, and established Rules of Government, all Parts of a Community have not a Right to a Degree of Liberty and Property correspondent to the Constitution under which they live?

'Tis nothing to the Purpose to say, we should make an ill Use of this Liberty, for if the Law of God, and the Rules of Equity allow it us, we have a Right to it, and must [69] answer for the Misapplication of our Liberty (as Husbands do for theirs) to God alone.

In the New Testament the Wife is commanded to *obey her Husband*;* and the Husband to *love his Wife:* And the *latter* is recommended by a divine Allegory, even the Love of *Christ* to his Church: And enforced in the strongest Terms, those

* *Eph.* v. 24.

of giving himself for her; but equally left to their Wills, whether they would walk according to these Injunctions or not. From whence I infer, that by our Laws he should be under as strong Obligations to do his Duty, as she hers: And if there had been any Retrospect to the Commands of God, that they should not be broken, 'tis to be supposed, the same Care had been taken as to him, as there was as to her.

I shall conclude all with the Words of an Author,* once before quoted, to whom the whole christian World is indebted, and for whose Sake I heartily pray God to give him Life and Health, to finish that great Work, which he has so excellently well begun. His words tho' wrote upon a different Occasion, may yet be applicable here.

"Alas, the Severity of the Chastisement [70] no Way infers the Dignity of the *Scourge!* tho' they have said with the proud Boaster in *Isaiah* c. x. 13. *By the Strength of my Hand I have done it, and by my Wisdom, for I am prudent: I have removed the Bounds of the People, and have robbed their Treasures, and as one gathereth Eggs that are left, have I gathered all the Earth; and there was none that moved the Wing, or opened the Mouth, or peeped:* Yet may we reply upon them with the Prophet, *shall the Ax boast itself against him that heweth therewith? As if the Rod should shake itself against them that lift it up; as if the Staff should lift up itself, as if it were no Wood.*"

FINIS.

---

* Preface to the second Volume of *Revelation examined, &c.* p.47. [Chapone concludes with the penultimate paragraph of the preface to volume two of Delany's *Revelation Examined.*]

Notes

1 The correct citation Psalm 55.

2 Page references here in the original.

3 The Court of Equity, or Chancery, was a court in London presided over by the Lord Chancellor that served as a counter to the courts of the common law, often acting to mitigate the harshness of the common law and developing its own jurisprudence particularly in the areas of trusts and guardianships.

4 Matt. 7:12. "Therefore all things whatsoever ye would that men should do to you, do ye even so to them: for this is the law and the prophets."

5 Petty treason was the crime of murder by someone in a subordinate position; of a master by a servant, of a husband by a wife. The punishment for the latter until 1790 was burning at the stake.

6 A "fine" was a legal procedure to transfer ownership of property, whereby the prospective owner would institute a lawsuit (real or fictional) in order to have the ownership of the land resolved.

7 Where a wife committed adultery ("criminal conversation") this was considered a civil, as well as a spiritual, injury and her husband could sue to recover damages. See William Blackstone, *Commentaries on the Laws of England, A Facsimile of the First Edition of 1765–1769*, vol. 3, *Of Private Wrongs* (1768), with an introduction by John H. Langbein (Chicago: University of Chicago Press, 1979), 139–140.

8 Lev. 19:3. "Ye shall fear every man his mother, and his father, and keep my sabbaths: I *am* the LORD your God." Additional support is found in Exod. 20:12, Deut. 21:18–21, Prov. 1:8, 6:20, Eph. 6:1–2, and Col. 3:20.

9 Wood, *A New Institute of the Imperial or Civil Law* (1730), 123, slightly misquoted.

10 This Objection is not included in the list in the Contents page; due to an error in the text (*Obj.* VI is repeated) the numbering is off until *Obj.* VII.

11 Psalm 124, "2. If it had not been the LORD who was on our side, when men rose up against us: 3. Then they had swallowed us up quick, when their wrath was kindled against us."

12 Jer. 10:24, "O Lord, correct me, but with judgment; not in thine anger, lest thou bring me to nothing."

13 William Shakespeare, *Macbeth*, 1.7.

14 The Book of Revelation includes several references to God and Christ ruling with a "rod of iron"; see 2:27, 12:5, 19:15. The first book of Kings alludes to chastising with scorpions in 12:1 and 14.

15 Wisd. of Sol. 11:16. "That they might know, that wherewithal a man sinneth, by the same also shall he be punished." The Book of Wisdom was part of the Apocrypha bound between the Old and New Testaments of the Authorized Version until the late nineteenth century.

16 Rom. 6:16: "Know ye not, that to whom ye yield yourselves servants to obey, his servants ye are to whom ye obey; whether of sin unto death, or of obedience unto righteousness?"

17 A slight, and interesting, revision of Luke 14:11, "For whosoever exalteth himself shall be abased; and he that humbleth himself shall be exalted." The passages echoes the Magnificat, where Mary marvels that despite "the low estate of his handmaiden," God has done for her "great things," and "exalted them of low degree," Luke 1:46–55.

18 2 Sam. 12:31, "And he [David] brought forth the people that were therein, and put them under saws, and under harrows of iron, and under axes of iron, and made them pass through the brick-kiln: and thus did he unto all the cities of the children of Ammon." The children of Ammon were David's enemies; Chapone is arguing that the harsh consequences under the English law for women are incommensurate and inequitable.

19 Gen. 3:19, Adam's punishment is to be expelled from Eden and consigned to a life of labor on earth, ending in death; "In the sweat of thy face shalt thou eat bread, till thou

return unto the ground; for out of it wast though taken: for dust thou art, and unto dust shalt thou return."

20 Ezek. 18:25, "Yet ye say, The way of the Lord is not equal. Hear now, O house of Israel; Is not my way equal? are not your ways unequal?" See also Micah 6:8, "He has shewed thee, O man, what is good; and what doeth the LORD require of thee, but to do justly, and to love mercy, and to walk humbly with thy God?"

21 Eph. 6:4. "And, ye fathers, provoke not your children to wrath: but bring them up in the nurture and admonition of the Lord."

Part Two

Remarks on Mrs. Muilman's Letter to the Right Honourable the Earl of Chesterfield.

In a Letter to Mrs. Muilman.

Remarks on
Mrs. Muilman's Letter
to the Right Honourable
the Earl of Chesterfield.

In a Letter to Mrs. Muilman.

Madam,

I have your Letter of the 5th of *April* now before me: Tho' the Court and Compliment is paid to Lord *Chesterfield*, it is apparently address'd to the Public, and
was originally design'd for the Press. You are pleas'd to acknowlege [sic] in your
Letter, Page 36th, that "every Reader is superior to a Writer; and that they are all
vested with natural Power of applauding or blaming, as they are inclined." As I
have taken the Liberty to make use of that Power as a Reader, I now refer myself
to your Judgment, and that of the Public, as a Writer; a Character I am so little
[4] fond of, that for that Reason, and no other, I must beg Leave to conceal my
Name. I shall very readily acknowlege my Motives for acting in a Character I don't
care to assume, and for which, I am really conscious, I am very slightly qualified,
except it be by the Love of Truth, and by Benevolence of Heart; two such absolute
Requisites, both in Writing and real Life, that the most shining Talents cannot make
a sufficient Amends for the Absence of either of these Qualities.

My first motive is a Christian, and consequently a Tender, Concern for your
Welfare.

My Second, that Regard which all Persons ought to bear to the Good of the Public.

As you are a most abused injured Woman, you have my affectionate Compassion.

As your Person, and natural Talents, are estimable, you have my Esteem, as
far as Esteem can be paid to any Talents misapplied.

As you either impose upon yourself, or endeavour to impose upon the Public,
you shall have my Animadversions.

You attempt to say things plausible and pleasing; you artfully acknowledge
your Errors, and then exculpate yourself from them. You [5] bewail the Miseries
these Errors have drawn upon you, but not in the Language of humble Penitence,
which only can recover lost Esteem, from that Part of Mankind whose Esteem is
really valuable. You say, in p. 2. you "readily take Shame to yourself;" but that's
a Mistake: Shame had taken you, had claimed you as her own, and entangled you
on all Sides; and you struggle hard to extricate yourself, and endeavor to spread

abroad the Net, that you may find some Hole to creep out at; for what else can you mean, when you say, Page 33, "I have already mentioned the Impossibility which I know I labour against, were I to attempt any Justification of my own Character; for Prejudice was, and Passion still is, too mighty against me, for the Voice of Truth and Reason to be heard: And I know also, any String that is touched upon to sound my Praises, would be Discord to the Ears of a prejudiced World, whose Food is Calumny?" Metaphorical Expressions! but implying that the most detestable Passions and Appetites rage in the whole World, that is, in your Censurers, or they could not be gratified by such diabolical Food; the natural Consequence of which must be, that they ought to take Shame to themselves, as well as you.

But what is this Calumny, that disturbs you so strangely? I wish you would give us your Sense of that Word. I am at a loss to un- [6] derstand it, as applied to any of the Facts, as related by Mrs. *T. C. Phillips* of herself, and published by her to the whole World. Is it Calumny to read that Apology? or to form any Judgment of her Conduct, from the Accounts of it written by herself? Oh! but she tells us p. 35. that she "was vilified by the World, before she told, what Motives her Actions had been governed by." To this the World will answer, That it can seldom take Cognizance of the Motives by which People act; and that if the Action be bad, the Motives to it cannot be good; "That Men do not gather Grapes of Thorns, or Figs of Thistles."[1]

The World ought, indeed it does, make great Allowances for all the subsequent ill Conduct of Miss *Phillips*, who in the early Dawn of Life, with all her Innocence, Inexperience, and blooming Beauty about her, was ensnared into the Power of a Brutal Monster; a Violator first of her Person, and, in consequence of that horrid Act, a Corrupter of her Principles; if we may judge of her Principles (and there is no other way of judging of them, but) by her future Behaviour even to this Day; any-thing in the Letter now under Consideration to the contrary notwithstanding.

Forcibly to ruin a Creature so fair–to blot her tender Youth with vile Dishonour– to tarnish every native Excellence–to drive her out [7] of the Paths of Peace and Virtue, and dash her upon Destruction! shew, that he had an Heart as hard as Marble, and that the last Line and finishing Stroke of the Image of the worst Being had been drawn upon it. Supposing the Fact to be as represented in the Apology of Mrs. *Phillips* (and which, as she rightly observes in her Letter, has not been contradicted), that Man, whoever he was (for I don't pretend to say Who he was) can have no Right to complain, tho' all Mankind shunned him, as something disgraceful to human Nature: But that was not all; he abandoned her, with as little Pity, as he ruined her: Cruelty in the Abstract! Who can reflect upon the Man, without the highest Indignation, or upon the lost unhappy Woman, without the most bleeding Compassion! I own, I never read more Tear-compelling Lines than in This, and some Parts of Mrs. *Phillips*'s Apology: Tho', upon the Whole, I cannot be well-pleased with the Writer; I cannot, because I know I ought not; for, by her own Account, she persisted in the most wicked Course of habitual Sin. One Kingdom was too small for her to allure by her Enticements, and infect by her Example.

Through what a Labyrinth of the most gross Sensuality has she rambled! Sometimes the Assailed, and sometimes the Assailant; but always concurring the Guilt!

[8] But 'tis time to return to the Letter, our more immediate Subject: You say, Madam, p.2. "that you are conscious, that your Misconduct has not arisen from Ignorance, so much as a Thousand concurring unhappy Circumstances that have attended you." This I readily believe, and have looked back to your Apology, for the most pitiable and most deplorable Circumstance that could attend any young Woman; and which, together with many other concurring unhappy Circumstances, ought in Justice so far to plead for some Alleviation, that, while Reason and Virtue condemn your Actions, Charity has a falling Tear, in Compassion to the Agent.

There is a natural Light in the Understanding, which, as far as it goes, always leads us to Truth: There is also a Prejudice arising from our Passions, and vagrant Affections, which as constantly leads us into Mistake and Error. Were the Mind always influenced by the latter, we should never be in the Right in any of our Judgments; and if always by the former, we should never be in the Wrong: For we must not impute our Mistakes to any inbred Quality in the Intellect; for then false Judgments would be natural to it, and we must take up with the Sceptics, and doubt of every-thing, till our Doubts might so increase by Doubting, that each Individual might complain, like *Ana-* [9] *ximander* of old, that he had not sufficient Evidence to conclude there was in Truth any real Existence in the Universe, except himself. All things else might be but Appearances–Shadows–and Phantoms, for any thing, that could be proved to the contrary.

Now this natural Light, as soon as it is applied to judge of any Action, becomes a practical Dictate of the Understanding, and is called *Conscience*; an intellectual Light, or informing Faculty, which acts back upon the Soul, by its own Force and Efficacy, and upon the first Reflection, directs–admonishes–and influences us, in what we ought to do, and what we ought to avoid. This you were born to; and as little as you were indebted to a pious Education, or owed to proper and solid Instructions, this gave you all those restless Nights, and, the Moment your Eyes were turned inward, all those stinging Reflections you speak of in p. 7.

But still you say, "You went on, in Hopes of better Fate." Better Fate from what? From stifling and subduing the natural Power of Conscience, and by Deeds of thick Darkness to put out this natural Light, which shewed you, your Actions were evil? Is there any Merit in this Knowledge which you could not be with- out? or in this Compunction, which you could not fling off? You go on and say, [10] you "found yourself cheated and undone." Give me Leave to tell you, for a melancholy Truth, that if you were cheated then, you cheat yourself now, if you fancy any thing contained in your Letter is real Penitence.

Well, you soon found you were in the wrong Way: Why did you not turn back? Why, because you allege, "There is a cruel Bar against our unhappy Sex, when once they offend against Virtue's sacred Rule, which rigorously excludes us from every Degree of Fame, be our future Conduct ever so nice, or scrupulously regular." This is not true; one Offence succeeded by a nice scrupulously-regular Conduct, will not deprive a Woman of every Degree of Fame; the World will forget the Fault, and, in time, will class such a one with the most unoffending of the Sex. Of this I could give Instances within my own Knowlege, but that the Persons deserve better than to have their Names mentioned upon such an Occasion.

But still I own there is a Bar; but deny that this Bar is fashioned only by Custom: It has its Foundation in Reason and Nature. The whole Creation, animate and inanimate, feels the Effects of similar Qualities, which collect the former into their respective Societies, whether of rational Beings or Brutes. While the latter, the inanimate Parts of the Creation, are connected, cohere, and become distinct Bodies, [11] by the Force of this Law. There are certain Tendencies, and Principles of Union, in the moral World, very analogous to specific Qualities in the natural World, from whence the thing is denominated to what it is: Hence arose that old Aphorism, "Shew me his Company, and I will shew you the Man." Nature or Reason dictate, that People of like Dispositions should keep together, because they cannot but chuse–delight in–and love each other. Nay, further, they will be insensibly drawn to imitate those they converse with, and love. He who engages the Attention, and influences the Affections of another, must in the same Proportion incline the Will; and the Will is the executive Power, which determines all a Man's Actions. The Understanding may perceive, and the Judgment direct, but the Will is the ruling, because the chusing, and, consequently, the accountable Faculty, in all free Agents. 'Tis therefore of the utmost Importance to all Persons, who design and desire to lead virtuous christian [*sic*] Lives, that their Companions should give sufficient Testimony, that they have not, or at least, will not for the future, allow themselves such Liberties as are absolutely inconsistent with the Principles of the Christian Religion. No one has any Right to complain and expostulate, that she is not publicly countenanced, whilst under the Imputation of such Practices, as are forbidden by the public Laws, both Ecclesiastical and Civil.

[12] I very readily acknowlege myself well-pleased with your Understanding, which, tho' not well improved, is excellent in itself. The Ill-treatment you have suffered from three Wretches, one after another, awakened my Pity, which engages me to give you this Testimony of my hearty Wishes for your thorough Reformation; and to assist you in it, according to the best of my Abilities. And in order to this, you must permit me to point out your Mistakes.

I think you never could be guilty of a greater Mistake in the Judgments you may have made of yourself, than when you say, p. 10. "To have been Mistress to an Emperor I should always have looked upon as a State of Infamy, Misery, and Dependence, to which I should have esteem'd the humblest Condition of Innocence that can be imagined, infinitely preferable." What hindered you, then, from extricating yourself from those Labyrinths of Vice in which you were entangled? A very small Portion of that Wealth which you squandered, when you made your boasted genteel Figure abroad, and which you also lavished upon your Vanities at home, might have made a virtuous reasonable Woman, easy in her Circum-stances, far from flinging her into the humblest Condition that can be imagined.

Besides, this humblest of Conditions was always in your Power, had it been in your Choice.

[13] But still you insist upon this cruel Bar as a Plea for remaining where you were. From what did this Bar preclude you? Not from repenting of your Faults, and living a virtuous Life. Be assured, Madam, nobody ever really reformed, but upon Principle. The Motives of Pleasure and Profit only vary their Temptations, when they persuade us to be virtuous, solely upon the Strength of worldly Inducements; and which, upon Experience, have ever been found to give Way, when any favourite Passion, or darling Inclination, pressed hard for their present Gratification. Prudential Considerations are allowed to be a good additional Fence to the Innocent, as sweet flowery Banks may direct the Course of a River, whose peaceful Waters glide on in even Majesty; but how weak and insignificant would they be to check a Torrent roaring loud, and rolling on, with impetuous Fury? So wild, and so uncontroulable, is the Tide of vagrant Affections! Now swaying this Way, now that, till all the Passions break over the Boundaries of Reason and Religion, and are as a Judgment let loose upon the Man, to worry him with still increasing Fury! "For wherewithal a Man sins, therewith shall he be punished."[2]

I agree with you, that this Bar may have put many a deluded young Woman upon sanguinary Acts of Cruelty and Desperation, to hide her Shame, and escape the Censures of [14] this World; but 'tis evident, that at that time she could have no Regard to the Horrors of the next. She is greatly the Object of Pity; but our Hopes of her Amendment, should she escape Discovery, can be but small, as she seems to have no Principles firm enough to bear the Weight of Repentance and Reformation.

Take away this Bar, and you let in a Torrent of Vice upon us, which at the same time that it may bear away Thousands of Innocents, will but confirm and strengthen the Guilty. It might indeed prevent those sanguinary Acts of Cruelty you so justly hold in Abhorrence; but it would encourage and increase the most gross Sensuality, which portions out Diseases and Death, and prepare accountable Creatures for final Perdition. Yet this is what you plead for in p. 13. and extorted that most shocking Wish (in such Circumstances, and upon such Motives) to change your Sex; tho' by such Change you "put on Ugliness and Deformity." There never was any thing so ugly, and so deformed, as that Wish, if we consider the Person and Inducements of her who made it. The Inducement follows in these Words; "Did Custom countenance us in the accidental Sallies of our Youth, and they were to be forgotten as in Men, I could vie with the most prudent of your Sex, for the Regularity of my Conduct, for these many Years; and for [15] the moral Part of it, always." Accidental Sallies of Youth! Why had you not said, obligeing [sic] Compliances –becoming Frolicks–and graceful Extravagances? Expressive of the Ardors of that gay Season of Life, its proper Ornaments and Praise! I must take the Liberty to insist upon it, that these Words might, with as exact Propriety, have been used as the other. Accidental Sallies! to what? Why, to the Regions of unutterable Sorrow, if God, in his unmerited Mercy, gives not the Grace of Repentance to such Salliers. "Forgotten, as in Men!" Then, with the Woman, described by *Solomon*, you would wipe your Mouth, and say, "I have done no mischief."[3]

What your Conduct has been I know not, but from your own Accounts. I read your Apology once, and no more, with such a Mixture of Pity, Terror, and Abhorrence, that I can never do my Heart the Violence of a Reperusal: Neither can descend to Particulars–The Detail were shameful! Yet, for the moral Part of this Life of yours, you say, you could always vie with the most prudent of the other Sex. God forbid! that none of the superior Sex should own the Obligations of, and live up to, the sacred Laws of Chastity! It were then better and safer for us to disband from Society, to suffer all the Inconveniences of the most solitary-unprotected Condition, rather than mingle in such dirty Community.

[16] First to publish a Life, so polluted, foul, and blotted; so wide in its Progress of Sin; so wasting, and so extravagant! and then, to vaunt of Purity of Morals, and private Virtues; of private Virtues in such Perfection, "that writing your private Life, would look too much like writing your own Panegyric;" is a Degree of Audacity (to say no worse) that I verily believe, has not been equalled in any Christian Country. Be so kind to give us a System of these Morals. I fansy, it must be as curious and singular, as this Boast, which has given the World some Right to demand it.

It has been laid down for a Rule, by a great and pious Author, "That it is not sufficient for a virtuous Mind to be innocent of the Evils it beholds."[4] All who love Virtue, in its true and proper Sense, must be alarmed when any Effort is made, tho' ever so weak, that attempts to sap its Foundations.

Morality is, on all hands, owned to be essential to true Religion. But it has been cried up of late, not only in Contradistinction, but to the Exclusion of all evangelical Graces, as if nothing more than what is prescribed by the dry mathematical Moralist were necessary to Salvation; and so, in Effect, rendering the Religion of JESUS CHRIST unnecessary, fruitless, and insignificant. It need not be said, that too much Success has attended these mischievous [17] Endeavours: Yet still they left us some Idea of moral Rectitude, and the Beauty of Virtue. 'Tis true, her Air was cold, philosophic and unaffecting; she could promise but little, and nothing with any Certainty, nor afford any Assistance towards the Attainment of these small uncertain Promises; yet, I say, they left us an Idea of moral Excellence, as something complete in all its Parts, without which there can be no Beauty: But if Mrs. *Phillips* has always lived a moral Life, why, we must lose the very Idea of Morality; at least till she is pleased to oblige us with her System, and instruct us how to reconcile her Actions to it.

You go on still bitterly complaining in p. 14. of this cruel Custom, which, you insinuate, would even out-face Demonstration itself; tho' I think the private Virtues, or private Life, of either Man or Woman, will hardly admit of demonstrative Evidence; Demonstration being the utmost Degree of mathematical Certainty, that the human Mind is capable of receiving: Nay, 'tis a kind of Infallibility; for whatever is demonstrated to be true, cannot possibly be false. Now if you will demonstrate, what at present you in great Modesty only "hint at," I will engage, the World shall believe you, and you shall incontestably regain all the Honour you have lost, and be self-recommended, and self-introduced to the Company or Conversation both of Men and Women, who, having most [18] Honour themselves, are most capable of conferring Honour on you, and all others.

You must be allowed to have just Grounds for your Assertion, when you say, "There is no Law, divine or human, that countenances these Sort of Gallantries more in one Sex than in the other." You have an undoubted Right to expostulate against that partial Rule, by which, you say, the Men acquit themselves, and each other: For nothing can be a more exact Imitation, or rather Exemplification, of the Malice of the grand Enemy of Mankind, than first to draw a poor Creature into Sin, and then to reproach her with such Compliances, and triumph in her Destruction. Yet this is the common Practice of all Men, who are so abandoned as to be "even profligate in their Amours:" And how such Behaviour can be consistent with any Principles of Honour, is hard to conceive. Honour is defined (as far as it will admit of a Definition) by a most judicious Author, to be

–A sacred Tye; the Law of Kings;
The noble Mind's distinguishing Perfection;
Which aids and strengthens Virtue, where it finds her;
And imitates her Actions, where she is not.[5]

But such Behaviour is neither Virtue, nor her Adjunct, nor an imitation of Virtue: 'Tis the lowest Meanness; 'tis Deceit and Treachery; [19] the most despicable Vices of the most despicable Minds! Such, all the worthy Part of the other Sex, with whom I have had the Advantage of conversing, allow it to be; and that Chastity is as essential to a Man of true Virtue, as to a Woman of the same Character. And why should it not? since the same Laws both of God and Man, which require it of one Sex, enforce it upon the other, under the same Sanctions of Rewards and Punishments; and most odious Consequences of criminal Indulgencies attend both, from the Nature of things, exclusive of the Penalties of any positive Law concerning it. The various-accumulated Mischiefs, and dreadful Effects of irregular Passions in both Sexes, plainly imply the same moral Turpitude in both; and that neither can plead any Patent of Exemption from the complicated Evils which await such Practices, both in this Life, and that which is to come.

How ignoble and degrading are the Lives of these Men of Honour, as you call them, and as they affect to be called?[a] How quick [20] the Transition between

---

a   Whoever desires to see larger, and yet more minute Pictures of these Men of Honour, and of those who esteem them as such, may gratify their Curiosity by reading *Clarissa*, where they will be seen drawn at full Length, by the most masterly intellectual Painter, that has adorn'd this Age and Nation. See particularly Mr. Belford's Letter to Mr. *Lovelace*. Vol. III. page 243. "Neither are Gratitude and Honour Motives to be mentioned in a Woman's Favour, to Men, such as we are, who consider all those of the Sex as fair Prize, whom we can obtain a Power over. For our Honour, and Honour in the general Acceptation of the Word, are two things." In Vol. VI. *Sally Martin* thus addresses *Clarissa*, "Don't speak against Mr. *Lovelace*, Miss *Harlowe*: He is a Man I greatly esteem; and, 'bating he will take his Advantage, where he can, of us silly credulous Girls, he is a Man of Honour."

loving and loathing! between a stupid Listlessness, and all the Rage and Madness of cruel Jealousy! For where there is no Virtue, there can be no Reliance. Quarrelling, Sickness, Pain, Distaste, Remorse, and a splenetic Restlessness ever attend the pitiful Circle of their little fleeting Amusements; till the languid, pale Remains of the giddy, ignorant, gaudy, empty Creatures, look like the very Ghosts of departed Pleasure, and are some of the most mortifying Spectres the human Eye can behold. Yet these Phantoms set up for Men of Fashion, and Men of Honour; and our poor deluded Sex are taught to respect them as such: Hence that most destructive and senseless Saying, "That reformed Rakes make the best Husbands." Supposing this true (which neither Reason, Experience, nor Religion, will allow); where is the Criterion, by which we can judge, they are certainly reformed? It is to be feared, the Vanity of our Sex has contributed to this Delusion. A young Creature is told by her Lover, and her Glass, that she has Charms to fix Inconstancy itself. [21] She also fondly thinks her own Prudence and Virtue must have a resistless Influence, even upon an Heart, where neither the Promises, or the Threats, of the living GOD have had any Effect. To this may be added, that all Men, who allow themselves to transgress this way, are most forward to insinuate, if not assert, that Chastity is not to be expected in Men; so that a young Woman is taught to think she has no Chance to find an unblemished Character in that respect; and therefore neither enquires or thinks about it; but fatally resigns herself to the Dissolute, as he may come recommended by Title, Equipage, or Fortune. As fruitful a Source of Evil as any in this wretched Earth! And to which nothing has so greatly contributed, as that Prejudice in favour of this Vice in Men, which your Letter tends to strengthen and confirm.

Many evil Examples first created this Prejudice, and then flattered and upheld it, till Vice became fashionable; and those who reverenced Virtue in their Hearts, durst not profess a proper outward Regard for it; so that the rising Generation must be prepossessed in favour of Vice, and the Charms of Virtue must grow fainter, and her Influence weaker, even upon those Hearts, who once felt her resistless Force, when recommended, and made visible in her native Beauty, by the Lives and Examples of wise and pious Christians.

[22] And can you wish, Madam, to see your own Sex reduced to as low a Standard of despicable Meanness? That we should all herd together, the clean and the unclean? That there should be no distinguishing upon Characters, but that all should be admitted and received alike? The very direct Method to bring us all to think and behave alike. A true Penitent is really a laudable Character; and when any Woman has given sufficient Testimony, that she is so, she has just Pretensions to regain the Esteem of the World; and it is to be hoped she would not be long without it; unless perhaps, from some few petulant Spirits, who may delight in invidious Reflections.

Yet, after all, it must be acknowleged, that sometimes a poor unhappy Creature may be inclined to return to the Road of Virtue, could she gain a ready Admittance to the Company she had unfortunately forsaken; and that this Difficulty may check this good Inclination. Yet still 'tis but Inclination, than which nothing is more variable. 'Tis not Reason and Religion; which would produce a vigorous Resolution to be virtuous for the future, tho' she might not attain all the outward Advantages and Honours due to that Character: For a Person influenced by Reason and Religion would know, "that the solid Joys of a good Conscience are solid Honours–solid Glory."[6]

[23] The Yet-untainted deserve and demand our first Care: 'Tis a more commendable Charity to preserve their Innocence from Infection, than it would be, to admit the Guilty in hopes of their Reformation. And I congratulate my Sex, that, in this most degenerate Age, there is yet some outward Regard for Chastity preserved amongst them. It may be laid down for a Rule, That so long as a Woman thinks it necessary to be virtuous herself, and determines, by the Grace of God, to continue so; so long she will be even nice and scrupulous in the Choice of her Company; and withdraw from those who, appear to act upon other Principles; or rather indeed, upon no Principles at all.

You go on with your very just Complaints (as they are supposed to be) against some of the other Sex. In p. 16. you ask with a becoming Warmth, "Does any History furnish Three such Instances of distinguished Villainy in Men? Yet are their atrocious Crimes buried beneath an Heap of Wealth; and Custom favours their Actions to such a Degree, neither of them are despised, shunned, or neglected by the World; and Men associate with them, as tho' they stood as fair in the Records of Fame, as ever *Socrates* did." Now, supposing this to be true, permit me to ask a few Questions: Do you in your Conscience think, that this Indulgence is likely to give them a stronger Sense of their Guilt? [24] and consequently, to produce Penitence and Reformation? Does it not rather tend to harden them in it? and being well received in this World, to put off all Thoughts of the Account to be given in another? The Misfortune and Unhappiness, of these unequal Measures of judging, lie on the Side of the Men; they guard Us, but betray Them into the most fatal Delusions; and "in fine, this Evil is pregnant with almost every Misfortune which happens to" the Men, but not to "us." 'Tis true, they are unjust to us, by such partial Rules of judging; but they are absolutely cruel to themselves; and the grand Mischiefs, the Mischiefs of Sin, and the Mischiefs of Punishment, will fall on their own Heads.

But farther, in p. 17. "Were returning Virtue to be rewarded with the Favour and Approbation of the World, you would soon see it crouded with Penitents of this Sort; and it would be giving our Sex an Opportunity of convincing you, they are not inferior to yours, either in Virtue, or Purity of Morals, when once they arrive at an Age capable of judging for themselves." GOD be praised! these are Points, which don't now remain to be proved! No Man, in his Wits would form his Opinion of the Sex, from the Behaviour of Children; that is, judge of Women, before they are Women; or deny so notorious a Truth, as that our Sex are not infe-[25] rior to theirs in Virtue, and Purity of Morals. What! can the Charms and Graces of Virtue be rendered becoming, only by those who had once forsaken her? Can she receive no Attestation from them who ever held her in Honour, and claimed her as the most distinguishing Privilege and highest Dignity of their Nature? Can Purity of Morals be only evinced by those who had lived to the Disgrace of all Morals? Indeed, Madam, we are not obliged to you for this Paragraph, by any means; we are ready to extend our Compassion, and charitable Assistance, for the Reformation of the guilty Part of our Sex; but want not a Reunion to establish our Characters in general, in the Opinion of the other Sex.

I can hardly think you so ignorant as you seem in p.18. when upon this Point you address the Men, as the Law-makers. Surely you must know, that the Laws of Chastity are of eternal Obligation; that they are the Laws of the universal Legislator; and that He only can "affix eternal Infamy," as a Punishment for the Breach of his own Laws.

You can't take the Abuse of Principles to be Principles themselves; nor think the Men decree, by a Law, the unequal Judgments they make of their own Sex and ours. In that cruel unequal Custom they have introduced, they rather act in a pontifical than a legislative Cha- [26] racter; they (as far as in them lies) dispense with the Divine Laws to support their carnal Tyranny; as the Pope takes upon himself, sometimes, to dispense with the same Laws, to support his spiritual Tyranny.

The whole Sex have a Right to expostulate upon this unequal Custom; but all who love Virtue would not wish a Remedy by taking the Restraints off our Sex; but would wish the same Restraints laid upon theirs, and that for their own sakes.

In p. 20. you say, "I have lived long enough in the World to despise it; I have sought for a Friend till I am tired with the Search."

What do you despise in the World? the Pomps and Vanities, of which you yourself have had so large a Share? And of which you boast but a few Lines above?–You intimate a Comparison, in more Places than one, in your Letter, between a very great Man and Yourself. If he went abroad to do Honours, you went to receive them. Honours were the Business, it seems, which employed you both, but not alike graceful in both; because not alike suitable to your respective Pretensions. You both roam about your Gardens: His Garden is his Choice; yours, your Refuge. Your Refuge, from a World, you say, you "look down upon." But what are the Heights that so exalt you? Have [27] Innocence and real Worth set you so far above the World, or the eminent Services you have done it? True Penitence can never admit of such Flights of Conceit as these, which are very inconsistent with the humble Airs you gave yourself at setting out, when you profess you "take Shame to yourself."

No Wonder, you have searched in vain for a Friend. A Friend is the Gift of GOD. He only, who made Hearts, can unite them. He creates all those generous Sympathies in kind concurring Minds, which may be called a Sort of terrestrial Intuition; and then, by his Providence, brings Persons so qualified, and so affected, together; where they perceive the Truth and Reality of each other's Virtue, by something they find within themselves, something so attractive, as to create an Assimilation of Desires, and a Conspiration of Counsels.

Virtue is the only Basis of a lasting Friendship. There is nothing in this World besides, substantial enough to bear the Weight, nor steady enough to sustain the Confidence, which Familiarity and Friendship require. There is so much Levity in every habitual Sinner, that, at best, he can but be the Entertainment of some unthinking senseless Hours; and who would set his Heart upon such Endearments, which last no longer than a Phrensy, and which [28] must vanish as soon as a Man comes to himself again?

When Principles of Reason, Good-nature, and Religion, combine together, and make up a perfect Harmony between two Minds, and unite them in laudable worthy Pursuits, then is their Friendship secure, firm, and noble! But when Men have all the Brands of Infamy upon them, what Assurance can they give of their Fidelity? And where there is no Assurance, there can be no Reliance.

Friendship essentially requires, that it be between Two at the least; and there can be no Friendship, where there are not two Friends. Now all vicious Habits extinguish the very Relation between Friends; in which case a Person ceases to be a Friend, not from any Inconstancy in himself, but from Defect in the Object for his Friendship to exert itself upon. It is one thing for a Father to cease to be a Father, by the Death of his Son; and another, to cease to be a Father by withdrawing his Affections from his Son, and casting him off. By the Death of the Son, the Relation is at an End for want of a Correlate; and by the Vices of a Friend, the Relation is at an End for the very same Reason: The Man, indeed, may live; but the Friend is dead, to all Intents and Purposes. [28]

[29] When you qualify yourself to be a Friend, I hope and believe you will find one; till then you have no Right to complain.

However, you profess yourself contented, and consequently chearful, and in a State of Tranquility: And this brings me to a Part of your Letter, p. 22. which all worthy Hearts must approve; namely, "the supporting an only Sister, and her little Family." This does you real Honour, and none ought, or indeed can detract from the Merit of it. I assure you, Madam, I have the Satisfaction to hope, that I am one of the last Persons breathing, who would knowingly and willfully detract from your Merit, or that of any other. Yet you must permit me to examine your Method of educating your young Niece, because you say, "In that will be best described your Sentiments of the true Duty of Woman."–You certainly lay a very proper Foundation "in the Love and Fear of GOD, as the first Principle, on which her every other Happiness depends." You are also in the right in your Censures of the modish Way of teaching young Ladies this first of Duties. The ignorance you deplore in these Points, it may be feared, is too general in both Sexes.

You declare, p. 23. that in either Sex, "when they have not real Religion, by which," you say, "I don't mean any particular Cult, [30] "but the true Love and Fear of God, there can be no moral Virtue." Then you always had this true Love and Fear of GOD; for you have already asserted, that the moral Part of your Life was always good; and now say, that moral Virtues can spring from no other Principles. You were less assuming in p. 21. for there you say, "Reason disapproves, and that I stand even self-condemned." And in p. 29. "For my Part, my Life has been one continued Scene of Error, Mistake, and Unhappiness." How is this consistent with the Purity of Morals, and the private Virtues, you so often talk of?

I am forced to skip backwards and forwards in this manner, to pursue you in your Doublings and Windings, in order to draw your Readers out of the Labyrinth, in which your fallacious way of Writing might involve them, and so entangle them in a Streight between Wickedness and Nonsense; for all Sin is Folly, and all Folly is Inconsistency.

By "any particular Cult," must be understood, any particular Persuasion in Religion, Mode, or Form of Worship, expressive of this "true Love and Fear of GOD." Any Mode, or Form, of Christian Worship, then, is no Part of your System. There can be no Christian Faith without Christian Worship: So the Articles of the Christian Faith are also out of the [31] Question. You find Fault with the modish way of teaching young Ladies: Yet you must teach your Pupil the modish Religion, or none, the modish Religion of Deism, or natural Religion. You profess, at your first setting out, to write the whole Duty of Woman; and when you take Leave of the Subject, in p. 33. declare you have done so, "as far as it comes within your Comprehension."[7] Indeed you modestly acknowlege, "There may be great Amendments made, and that several necessary Hints may be given towards the rendering your System complete." Yet still you call it a System, tho' you allow, that, perhaps, it may not be absolutely complete. Now there never was a System of the Christian Religion (which only can teach a Christian Woman her Duty) without Faith in JESUS CHRIST. Therefore yours is not a System of the Christian Religion, or a System drawn from the Principles of the Christian Religion; for you don't once mention Faith in JESUS CHRIST, as any Part of the Duty of Woman. Well then, it must be natural Religion you would teach. Let us see what this natural Religion would do for you, as a Person whose "Reason disapproves her past Actions, and stands even self-condemned." What must such Sinners do? Repent, you'll say; for "'Tis agreeable to the Goodness of God, to accept Repentance, and restore Offenders to his Favour. Very well. But how often will this Remedy serve? May Sin and Repent- [32] ance go on for ever in a perpetual Round? To allow this, differs nothing from allowing a Liberty and Impunity to Sin, without Repentance. If GOD is Judge and Governor of the World, there must be a time for Judgment; and Men may, after all reasonable and equitable Allowances made, be ripe for Judgment. Let this be the Case then: Suppose a Man, after all equitable Allowances made, to be condemned under and by the Law of Nature; and living in daily Expectation of Execution. I ask, What Sort of Religion you would advise him to, in the mean time?–Natural Religion?–To what purpose? He has had his Trial and Condemnation by that Law already, and has nothing to learn from it, but the Misery of his Condition. I do not mean, that the Sense of natural Religion will be lost in such a Man. He may perhaps see more clearly, than ever he did, the Difference between Good and Evil, the Beauty of moral Virtue, and feel the Obligations a rational Creature is under to his Maker. But what Fruit will this

Knowlege yield? What certain Hope or Comfort will it administer? A Man with a Rope about his Neck may see the Equity and Excellency of the Law, by which he dies; and if he does, he must see, that the Excellency of it is to protect the Virtuous and Innocent: But what is this Excellency to him, who has forfeited the Protection of all Laws? If you would re- [33] commend Natural Religion, exclusive of all other Assistance, 'tis not enough to shew from Principles of Reason, the Excellency and Reasonableness of moral Virtue, or to prove from the Nature of GOD, that he must delight in, and reward Virtue. You must go one Step farther, and prove from the Nature of Man too, that he is excellently qualified to obey this Law, and cannot well fail of attaining all the Happiness under it, that Nature ever designed him for. If you stop short at this Consideration, what do you gain? What imports it, that the Law is good, if the Subjects are so bad, that either they cannot, or will not, obey it? When you prove to Sinners the Excellency of natural Religion, you only shew them, how justly they may expect to be punished for their Iniquity. A sad Truth, which wants no Confirmation! All possible Hope left in such a Case is, that GOD may freely pardon and restore them; but whether he will or no, the Offenders can never certainly learn from natural Religion.

"Should GOD think fit to be reconciled to Sinners, natural Religion would again become the Rule of their future Trial and Obedience; but their Hopes must flow from another Spring: Their Confidence in GOD must, and can arise only from the Promise of GOD; and we have no Promise of Re- [34] conciliation for Sinners, but through the Merits and Mediation of CHRIST."[8]

You will pardon me, Madam, this long Quotation, since it seems so very apposite to your Case. And the Author is of so great Authority, that for Soundness of Arguments, and Solidity in the Application of them, he is generally esteemed second to no Man in the Kingdom. If you should chuse to see what he says farther, it may be worth your while; at least, I never employed any time more to my Improvement and Delight, than in reading the Works of this all-illuminating Author. He casts such a Light upon every Subject, that it must be owing to the Blindness or Perverseness of his Readers, if they are not the wiser and the better for him.

The Quotation is taken from, *The Use and Intent of Prophecy, in the several Ages of the World.*

Natural Religion seems, then, to be insufficient in the present State of human Nature. If so, your Instructions must be very defective, since you teach no other. You have indeed very judiciously furnished your Pupil with Two very proper Books, as you tell us in p. 29. *Telemaque* and Dr. *Tillotson*, both of them, for her moral Instruction.[9]

[35] *Telemaque* may be called the Continuation of an Epic Poem, notwith-standing it is written in Prose. Yet the Style is raised above common Prose, and animated with such Fire, that it speaks the Language of Poetry, abounding in Metaphor and Rapture, and painting every Idea with a Tincture of the Muses. The

admirable Author designed to form the Manners of his Readers, by the Instructions he gives to his Hero, in the Person of *Mentor*; who, at length, appears to be no less than *Minerva*, the Goddess of Wisdom, herself; intending to shew his Readers, after this allegorical manner, that true Wisdom can come only from the Gods. In order to this, he makes use of the proper Machinery of an Epic Poem, which allows the Poet to bring some Deity, or supernatural Being, upon the Stage, either to solve some Difficulty, or to perform some Exploits, beyond the Reach of Human Power.

Now supposing a young Girl, quite uninstructed in the Truth, and great Importance, of the Articles of the Christian Faith; and *Telemaque*, and Dr. *Tillotson*, were both put into her Hands by her Preceptor, with Directions to learn Morality from them both; is it likely she would think her Preceptor designed she should believe any more in JESUS CHRIST than in *Mentor*?

[36] The sacred Writings, tho' by far the noblest, and most sublime, this World was ever enlightened with, are not once mentioned. 'Tis true, you say, p. 23. "I can very soon bring myself to conceive what that Man or Woman's Actions must be, who have no Dependence upon future Reward or Punishment."

But whether you believe the Doctrine of future Rewards and Punishments, as Articles of the Christian, or Natural Religion, you are not pleased to declare. And this Ambiguity appears rather like a Covert for an Author to retreat to, than any Explanation to a Reader, who is to judge of her Principles. Besides, there are many presumptive Circumstances through the Whole of your Instructions, which seem too much designed to form your Pupil, merely as a Creature of this World.

A very charitable and candid Reader may be permitted to entertain some Suspicions, that a Writer might intend those Inferences, which her Doctrines so plainly suggest.

I would not from hence infer, that you believe nothing of future Rewards and Punishments, or of another Life; but that your Understanding and Desires long have been, and still are, so engaged and entangled in the Pleasures and Pursuits of this Life, that you have neither [37] Talents nor Inclination to give such Rules and Instructions, as bear a steady Eye to the Happiness of the next; and consequently, that your System by no means contains the whole Duty of Woman; that is, of a reasonable, accountable, immortal Being.

You have the other Sex continually in your Eye, in all your Documents. You propose their Approbation as the Reward of all your Pupil's Attainments. You tell her, p. 27. "That there is no other Way to make herself happy, but by endeavouring to cultivate those lasting Accomplishments of which MEN never tire."

Pleasing the Men is here proposed as the first Spring, and ultimate End, of all her Endeavours: As "a well-taught honest Mind" may contribute to this great End, you recommend it, in the very next Line. A Person of a better Turn would have recommended it, upon a better Motive than this; which is enough to turn the very Brains of a young Girl, by giving a wrong Byas to her Inclinations and Pursuits, which must be necessarily bent and drawn towards the Men, as she is taught her

Happiness depends solely on them. Hence, she may learn an artful Carriage; and to form the Exterior according to the rules you have laid down; but as she will soon know, that Men cannot be Searchers of Hearts, will never give her Simplicity of [38] Mind; a Virtue of such Perfection, that, if I may so speak, it realizes all others; since no Man can be assured even of the Truth and Reality of his own Virtue in any Point, farther than he is assured of his own Simplicity.

As a Creature born for Society, [a] great Part of your Niece's Happiness must depend upon the Reception, Favour, and Approbation, she will find in Society. She should therefore be taught to qualify herself for the Society of the Wise and Virtuous, whose Favour and Approbation, only, are worth the having, or valuing herself upon; and which only can be enjoyed with Safety to her own Morals and Character. This might give her a right Judgment of things, and instruct her to value People as she finds them good or bad; not as she considers them as Men and Women. The less a young Girl is led into such Reflections, the better; and, indeed, there is little Occasion for them: For I must tell you, Madam, (as a Truth you may have had little Opportunity of knowing), that in the Company of Women of true Modesty, and real Virtue, all those Decencies, and even Delicacies, which give a Dignity to the Sex, are as constantly preserved amongst ourselves, as when the Men croud our Drawing-rooms. You may be very sparing, therefore, in your particular Directions, concerning the young Lady's Behaviour towards the other Sex, since general Directions will be sufficient upon all common Oc- [39] currences; provided she keeps proper Company and if she keeps improper Company, 'tis to be feared no Directions may be sufficient.

In your 5th Page you profess, you "have really an utter Detestation to any thing that has the least Shadow or Appearance of Flattery." Yet your 28th Page favours very strongly of that intoxicating Incense, which you there offer to the Men in general; with a Clause expressing great Resentment in favour of those honest Gentlemen, who may chance to be tormented with witty Wives. In short, you say, you have an utter Abhorrence of Wit at any rate, "unless, as in your Lordship, it is in a sensible good-natured Man's keeping: But, in a Wife, 'tis productive of many Ills." And why may not Wit be as useful and agreeable in a sensible, good-natured Woman's keeping? If GOD has been pleased to entrust her with that shining Weapon of Defence, it won't be in your Power, or any-body's else, to wrest it out of her Hands: No; nor by the most perverse Struggles to make it so much as cut her own Fingers. True Wit is Reason, in its gayest, most delightful, most instructive Strain. Such is Lord *Chesterfield*'s Wit allowed to be, by far superior Judges to myself. Such Wit would be the highest Ornament, and most charming Accomplishment, of the finest Woman in *Europe*. What Evils could Wit (barely as such) be productive of in a Wife? It might, [40] indeed, shew her, that her Husband was a Fool (supposing that to be really the Case), but not make him so. I agree with you, that this would be, not only a very dangerous, but a very disagreeable Situation, for a Woman; but not so dangerous for her, nor her Family neither, as if there were two Fools at the Head of it. But you certainly mistake Wit, for the Affectation of Wit. All Affectation is highly disgusting; but in no Point, more than in this; because none is so certain of Discovery upon the Spot. A Man might as easily impose upon his Company, by affecting to light up his Room of Entertainment with a Sun-beam at Midnight, as to assume and retain the Character of Wit, when he has it not; Wit, like the Sun-beam, being seen solely by its own Light; and being also as much above Imitation.

The indispensable Ornament of a Woman is Modesty, which will effectually suppress all those little pert Petulancies in Conversation, which, it may be supposed, you endeavour to explode, under the Notion of Wit. But this may be misleading a young Woman's Judgment, without reforming her Manners. For Wit ever was held in Admiration and Esteem; and if she takes these Flights of Conceit for Wit, you will have much ado to persuade her out of them. But if you shew her, that true Wit must, in the Nature of things, be the Effect of sound Judgment; and that no one, with [41] the least Degree of Judgment would wantonly expose, or disoblige her nearest and dearest Friend, her Guide, Guardian, and Protector, 'tis most likely, you might not only suppress that vain-glorious, ridiculous Spirit, but all other silly Humours, which might otherwise interrupt her domestic Peace.

'Tis to be supposed there never was a Woman (who was not incorrigibly a Fool, and so not worth the Reprehension) that ever flattered herself, that she did make a better Figure, for her Husband's being a Fool, or from his appearing to be so. I wonder what brought such a Conceit into your Head: You surely fansied it a pretty Introduction to the extraordinary Adulation, which follows, in very positive Terms: "I do insist upon it, the only one (Light) they (that is, Wives) can ever shine in, is that, which borrows its Lustre from their Husbands." Thank Heaven! all they borrow they easily repay with Interest, if the Authority of the wisest and greatest of Kings has any Weight; who says, "That a virtuous Woman is a Crown to her Husband;"[10] *i.e.* She is his Honour, Ornament, and most exalted Distinction. Indeed, where a Woman has no Honour of her own, she must borrow her Lustre from her Husband, if she will have any, and he happens to have any to lend; but if he has not (which you know may sometimes be the Case), they must both go without.

[42] In p. 30. we have a Catalogue of the Virtues, which this System of yours, you hope, will produce. I shall only say, I hope too, that the young Lady may attain all these Virtues in the highest Perfection; but, if they are produced by the Strength and Efficacy of this System of Education, it will be the first Instance of such an Effect, following from such a Cause, since the Fall of Man.

After having put the finishing Stroke to your System, you ask Lord *Chesterfield* to tell you, If he thinks it a good one? I find some People apprehend the Publication of this Question implies your having received an Answer in the Affirmative, previous to such Publication. And they are the rather inclined to this Opinion, because in p. 34. you inform the World, by telling Lord *Chesterfield*, in Print, that "Witticisms you never can fear, while his Lordship is pleased to condescend to be your Protector." Now, should this be the Case, and I should unhappily have given any Offence (tho' far from aiming at any Witticisms); and his Lordship should please to give a public Testimony of such Protection, which is the only way that Writings, of which all the World are in Possession, can be effectually protected; why, to confess the Truth, I should rather fall into the Hands of another Man. I have long reverenced Lord *Chesterfield* as a King in the Realms of Wit, Knowlege, and Eloquence; [43] but hope he won't turn Tyrant, and attempt to force us out of our antient legal Possessions; for I contend for no Truth, that we have not been in Possession of, above these Seventeen hundred Years; either by express Words in our Grants and Covenants, or from such Conclusions as necessarily follow from the Premises. Nothing but moral Force, *i.e.* superior Arguments, shall drive me out of these Entrenchments; which, as the Wit of Man did not raise, so, I trust, the Wit of Man shall never be able to render untenable.

As for what has been, or shall be, said of your Conduct and Character, I appeal, first to Mrs. *Phillips*'s Apology; and secondly, to Mrs. *Muilman*'s Letter: Authorities to which, 'tis apprehended, none can make any Exception.

When I read p. 14. this bitter Complaint, "There is neither Man nor Woman, by whose Company or Conversation I should think myself honoured, that would dare publicly countenance me," I little expected to find, p. 34. a Boast so inconsistent with this Complaint: You there claim the public Patronage and Protection of one of the greatest Men in the three Kingdoms; and, in a manner, threaten your Objectors (if such there should be) with *him*. If this is not publicly countenancing you, you certainly publicly countenance yourself, by his Protection; which is much the same thing. I [44] am persuaded you did not mean to insinuate any Reflection on my Lord *Chesterfield*; as if the public Countenance, he is pleased to afford you, could do you no Honour: But this is one of the many Inconsistencies which a good Understanding may be drawn into, when it has a bad Cause to defend. Its Business must be, to amuse, to talk plausibly; and, as Lord *Clarendon* phrases it, "to speak as near Reason, as any Man who does not speak Reason."

I don't apprehend, that, as a woman, you stand in any Relation to Lord *Chesterfield*; and how Obedience can be due, where there is no Relation, is hard to conceive. You tell Lord *Chesterfield*, p. 32. "To convince your Lordship, I thoroughly understand what that (the whole Duty of Woman) means in your Sense of it, I look upon Obedience to be a principal Part; in consequence of which, I have wrote your Lordship what I conceive the Duty of Woman to be." What! do all Women owe Obedience to all Men, as such? I will venture to say, that is not my Lord *Chesterfield*'s Sense of the Matter. He may have a Claim to your grateful Compliance in such a Point, as your generous Protector; but not merely as he is a Man, and you a Woman. Honour and Precedence is one thing, Jurisdiction and Authority, another. Neither Rank, nor Sex, confer any Right to claim Subjection and Obedience; which are only due in such [45] Relations of life, where the Laws of GOD have given a Right to demand them. An humble submissive Style is very becoming, when addressed to Superiors, upon all common Occasions; but is absurd, when it draws a Person in, to advance false Principles upon a Point of Duty of such Importance, that half the Species are concerned in it.

P. 34. you say, "The World has always been at War with me, under *Pretence* of my leading a blameable Life; I with them, for the Reasons I have given; and also, that there are but few of my Enemies, who do not apparently practise, themselves, the Vices they pretend to disapprove in me."

Vice is the only absolute, essential, uncompounded Evil in human Life. All other Evils may be so circumstanced, that they may possibly be productive of Good; but moral Evil, neither in itself, nor its Consequences, ever can become a Good, or productive of Good. No Wonder then, that even the Vicious themselves express Dislike and Horror at the Deformity of Sin, when they behold it, in its genuine Ugliness, in another. Some Sins of Intemperance even deface the Image of GOD in the human Countenance; and then the whole Creation affords not a more disagreeable Object. You complain of the Vices of others, because, you [46] say, you have been injured by them. As far as an evil Example reaches, so far the whole Community is injured; and consequently have the same Right to complain of you, who have set a very evil Example: Notwithstanding which you have the Audacity to say, the World is at War with you, under *Pretence* of your leading a blameable Life. After having declared you are in a State of Hostility with the World, you immediately add, "There are but few of my Enemies who do not apparently practise, themselves, the Vices they pretend to disapprove in me." If this is not Calumny upon the World in general, I know not what is so. 'Tis impossible you can prove the Charge you have made so very extensive. Then the World, it seems, maliciously *pretends* you have led a blameable Life; –brings a false Charge against you; and is therefore the Aggressor. How is this to be reconciled with many Acknowlegements and Confessions, already taken notice of in your Letter? In your Apology you publish very many, and very great Crimes of *Tartuff*; by which you yourself were not personally injured, farther than these Crimes were injurious to some People in the Community.[11] And you still threaten to publish more of *Tartuff*. What is it, that has rendered your Character so sacred, that the World may not take the same Liberty with you? If you commit Actions worthy of Blame, you have no Right to complain, that the World in general blames [47] you. True Penitence is far from that recriminating Spirit, which breathes in almost every Page of your Letter, and endeavours to blast all your Censurers with the odious Imputation of delighting in Calumny. You go on, p. 36. "Therefore, as, during my whole Life, I have been accustomed to the Mal-treatment of the World, whether deservedly or no, their Wit will lose its Edge on me."

'Tis to be feared, you may then be incorrigibly hardened against all Reprehension; and their Wit may lose its Edge, for the same Reason that a Razor would lose its Edge, were it applied to hew a Block.

The whole Creation produces nothing more impenetrable, than the Heart of an obstinate hardened Sinner.

But it may be hoped that is not your Case; and that you, Madam, will consider where you have done amiss, and make the best Reparation in your Power. Restitution you cannot make: For what Equivalent can be given to a Woman for the

Loss of her Peace of Mind; for the extreme Distress of herself and Children, while you detained her Husband from her? Your own Heart will point out Particulars of this kind; they need not be named, either to inform you, or the World, which has long contained many Wretches, which Mrs. *Phillips* has con- [48] tributed to make such. The Injured and the Innocent have many things to lay to her Charge in many Families, while she cajoled and plundered the unworthy Heads of them. Hence that "genteel Figure abroad;" and thus were "the Deficiencies of Fortune so amply supplied."

No one denies your having a Right to demand Justice of all those who may have injured you, and to do yourself that Justice (as far as lies in your Power) which they deny you. But state Accounts with the World in general, before you begin to draw upon Particulars; and then you will see what you have to demand in this Life, and what to expect in the next: A Matter of some Importance, and which not only demands, but will compel, your Attention to it, at a time when nothing can divert your Thoughts from it.

The Love of Pleasure is an Excuse, which you may plead in common with various Transgressors. The Sensualist, the Proud, the Cruel, the Rapacious, the Fraudulent, and the Avaricious, all pursue their several Pleasures. It may be supposed, that few on this Side the bottomless Pit have ever arrived to such a Despite of God and Goodness, as to chuse Sin, for its own sake; to love Vice barely as such, without any farther Incentive. The most powerful Temptations, which prevail on Men to [49] transgress human Laws, and deliver such Offenders up to the Justice of their Country, are generally founded in some natural Desire, which is therefore pleasurable; and upon that Account tempts, solicits, and entices the Will. For there is hardly one Vice, of direct and personal Commission, but what is the Irregularity and Abuse of one of those Two grand natural Principles; namely, either that which inclines a Man to preserve himself; or that which inclines him to please himself. But as no Arguments drawn from the Pleasure of the Transgression, would be pleadable in an human Court of Judicature, so as to obtain Exemption, or even Abatement of Punishment; so neither shall they have any saving Force or Efficacy before the unerring Judge, into whose Hands you must fall, and for whose Appearance you ought to prepare yourself by Repentance, and, by your future Life, to make the best Amends you can, for the Scandal you have given "in a Christian Country." Such you call it, in your Letter, when you would shelter yourself under those divine Principles of Charity, which Christianity teaches; yet in your System of Education you wholly omit every Christian Doctrine, as such, or as taught by the Dispensation of the Gospel.

It must be allowed, you express a very just and becoming Indignation at the trifling disgusting Treatment, you still find from the other Sex; and that with so proper a Spirit, and so [50] much good Sense, that whoever offends you that way for the future, must be unconvertibly stupid. Had you a just Life to defend, or had written in the humble self-abasing Spirit of true Penitence, perhaps few Writers could produce much better natural Talents. The Abuse of a good Understanding may possibly make you so crafty, that you may, in some degree, deceive youself.

'Tis certain you endeavor by Plausibilities to impose upon the Public; and as your Letter appears to receive some Sanction from the noble Lord, to whom it is addressed, it may possibly be attended with some ill Consequences.

First, As you would break down that Partition which, at present, separates those of our Sex who bear unblemished Characters, from those who do not; and so give the Vicious free Access to the Virtuous; than which nothing can be more dangerous to the latter, who from Merit, and I hope and believe, also from Numbers, deserve our first Care. There is such an alarming Connexion between Levity of Manners, and a total Disregard to Virtue itself, that whoever gives into the former, cannot assure themselves, nor the World neither, that they shall not be soon brought to the latter. Nothing is so likely to introduce universal Levity of Manners, as a free undistinguishing Admittance of all Company, without a proper Discrimination upon Characters. I said once before, [51] yet, to avoid Misconstruction, I repeat again, that a true Penitent is a worthy Character; and when any unhappy Offender shall have given sufficient Testimony, that she is a real Penitent, all the Laws of Humanity and Charity plead for her Re-establishment in the Favour and Esteem of the World; and it is cruel and unchristian to refuse her all those Marks of Respect, which were originally due to her.

Secondly, Your Letter insinuates and upholds false Principles, in respect of the other Sex; for you seem to allow, that Chastity is not to be required of Men in general; and therefore very modestly wish yourself one of them. In p. 14. you advance a false Fact in these subsequent Words: "You will all admit Men may be even profligate in their Amours, and none of you will dispute their being, in all other respects, Men of Honour; and, as such, they are admitted into all Companies, and by all Ranks and Degrees of People."

This is not true; for all the Wise and the Good of the other Sex, that is, every true Christian Man, does and will deny, "That Men may be even profligate in their Amours, and yet, in all other respects, Men of Honour;" taking Honour in any laudable Sense of the Word. The latter Part of your Assertion greatly wants Limitation: For tho' such Profligates may be sometimes admitted [52] into Company, by all Ranks and Degrees of People (taking Ranks and Degrees to signify no more than Stations in Life); yet, as bad as the World in general is thought to be, such Men never were the chosen Companions of any one truly estimable Man, of any Rank or Degree; and when they are suffered to invade the Houses of better Men than themselves, they are secretly despised, and neither beloved or trusted as Men of real Honour, nor receive farther Countenance than the outward Civilities of Conversation, which, it must be allowed, is far more than they merit; and which, in Reason and Religion, ought not to be granted them, and to which they can plead no Right, "but Custom, cruel unequal Custom!" Custom, which thus seems to countenance their Transgressions; and to which, it may be feared, many a one owes an hardened reprobate Heart;–the greatest Evil, and the severest Judgment, that can befal a reasonable accountable Creature, on this Side the Grave; whither we are all hastening, and from whence we can make no Retreat. Pass but a few more setting Suns, and, as far as they concern us, all things here, shall vanish with an everlasting Flight: All that boundless Vanity imagines, or wild Ambition craves, will then afford no Consolation for an infinite Good, departed, forfeited for ever! The soft Voice of Pleasure will no more insinuate and allure; nor the exalted Voice of Glory animate and inflame![12]

[53] It has been the Opinion of several Philosophers, that the Soul in her separate State may have many latent Faculties awakened in her, which she is not capable of exerting, in her present Union with the Body; and that these Faculties may, in all Probability, correspond with some unknown Attributes of the Deity, and open to her, hereafter, new Matter for Wonder, Love, and Praise. And, by Parity of Reason, we may be assured, that whatever new Faculties may spring up in the Soul, that her Capacity of receiving Pleasure will be her Capacity of admitting Pain; and that all her boundless Faculties shall by fully replenished with ineffable Delight in the next Life, or dreadfully expanded with unutterable Woe. The Soul must ever be so absolutely in the Power of its Creator, that he may raise such Horrors in it, to terrify it with such ghastly Apprehensions, as almost to fright it out of its own Existence, by most dreadful Impressions of the Anger of the living GOD. Shame and Fear are acknowleged to be the most painful Passions in the human Soul: They are both the genuine Offspring of Sin, and its proper and adequate Punishment; but as the human Mind cannot bear Shame or Fear, in their utmost Excess, without Distraction or Death, so no Words can fully describe them; but they shall be felt when all Words are vain, when Guilt, Shame, Fear, Despair, Rage, and Anguish, sink down the Soul, by their own Weight. Yet, [54] possibly, divine Vengeance may inflict upon it additional Sufferings, which the exalted Nature and Essence of the Soul may sharpen beyond all Conception; for the more delicate the Being, the more subtle its Perceptions, and the more exquisite the Torment. Every Man, by his own Experience, must find, that the Soul, whilst in the Body, feels many Pains and Pleasures, which both arise and terminate in itself, and which are of too refined and delicate a Nature to make their Abode in the Organs of Sense; but dwell in the inmost Recesses of the Mind:[13] Such as, the Trouble or Peace of Conscience, the Vexation or Delight of Mind, in the fruitless Search after, or in the Contemplation of, excellent and important Truths. Such is the vigorous Activity, and enterprising Nature of the Soul, even while clogged and retarded by these earthly Bodies, that it must ever be in Pursuit of something. If the Joys and Glories of Heaven are not its strongest Attractives, the Pleasures and Honours of the Earth will be so; and in that Point, few, if any, are satisfied with their Portion. When Death shall have cut the Cable, and shattered the Hulk of this frail Barque, the Body, it casts the sinful Soul upon an unknown Strand, naked, poor, and desolate, without Support, Friends, or Hopes; the dismal Blackness of eternal Night surrounds it; and conscious Guilt and Despair redouble the Horrors, and so thicken the [55] Darkness, that, to use the emphatical Words of Scripture, it may even be felt.

In vain does the Soul look back upon the Earth: That, and all its Splendors, are for ever vanished like a Dream; Rest is fled far away, with all its gaudy Attendants, of Pleasures, Honours, Beauty, and Ambition. The Soul may repeat ineffectual Wishes for the Body, the Medium by which it received its former Pleasures! But, alas! it hears the Voice of Joy no more! It lies dead, stiff, pale, and cold! 'Tis past the Power of Oratory, or the most alluring Charms, to awaken in it one single Glimpse of Desire, one imperfect Act of Life; till that tremendous Day, when the quickening, when the Dust-collecting Trump of God, shall rekindle Life and Activity, and call it to rejoin the Soul, in a new World, where every-thing will be strange, dreadful, unalterable, and eternal!

I beseech you, Madam, to let your Thoughts dwell a little upon these things; and to reflect whether it may not be more for your true Interest, to endeavour to make your Peace with GOD, than to trifle with the World, by indefensible Representations of the Purity of your Morals; and, by false Principles, to sap the Foundations of all Morality.

The Scandal you have given is public; your Apology (such a one as it is) is public; your [56] Letter is public: 'Tis fit therefore the Animadversions upon it should be public also: Otherwise, far be it from me to desire to add the least Grain to the Weight of your Reproach, or to aggravate your Misdoings.

As far as I can hear, your Letter is universally read; and, considering the Cause you had to defend, is skillfully written. You have the Art and Address to soften and please your Readers; and, by the Sallies of a lively Imagination, so to dazle [sic] the Understanding, that it does not instantly perceive the many Evasions, Misrepresentations, and Inconsistencies, that run through the Whole. However, you must pardon me, if I confess, that I should not have thought your Authority, either as a good Liver, or a good Writer, of such alarming Consequence, as to call for a public Refutation of whatever false or idle Principles or Notions you may have advanced; but, being in Company, and making Objections to some Parts of your Letter, a Gentleman replied (as a full Answer to all that could be said), "'Tis evident Lord *Chesterfield* approves what Mrs. *Muilman* has written. Doubtless he saw the Letter before it was printed; at least, all those Parts to which you object, as far as her Principles and his Patronage are concerned, must be supposed to have been communicated to him, before Publication; and his Lordship's Opinion will have great Weight with Mankind, who have [57] long been convinced of the Excellency of his Understanding."

As to myself, I take the Matter in another Light. I rather think, that Lord *Chesterfield's* Protection and Patronage were granted upon Motives of Compassion for a Woman, who had early been injured without any Reparation; nay, in Truth, beyond all Reparation. Motives of Esteem for the Talents you are Mistress of, might incline him to allow you to address your Letter to him, as it might promote the Sale of it; but without any Design to have it thought, he subscribed to all the Principles or Opinions it might contain. Should I be mistaken in his Lordship, and his Motives, I must take the Consequence; for I freely confess, that, had his great Name been wholly omitted, I should not have imagined, that your Opinions, barely as such, would have been likely to have had any strong Influence upon the Opinions or Practice of the Public, which has long, in general, expressed the highest Disapprobation of your Life and Manners.

While there is Life, there is time for Repentance; and when I am so happy as to hear you are a Penitent, upon Christian Motives and Principles, none shall be more ready to acknowledge your Merit, or be with greater Esteem,

Madam, Your most Obedient

July 2. 1750.   *Humble Servant.* [58]

Notes

1 Matt. 7:16. "Ye shall know them by their fruits. Do men gather grapes of thorns, or figs of thistles?"
2 Wisd. of Sol. 11:16. "You sent upon them swarms of dumb creatures for vengeance; that they might recognize that one is punished by the very things through which one sins."
3 Prov. 30:20. "Such *is* the way of an adulterous woman; she eateth, and wipeth her mouth, and saith, I have done no wickedness."
4 Chapone may be alluding here to the preface to Patrick Delany's *Revelation Examined* (Dublin, 1732), vol. 2. "Methinks it is but a poor consolation to a Christian spirit, to be innocent of the evils it beholds" (xxvi). ECCO. The preface was issued separately as *The Present State of Learning, Religion, and Infidelity in Great-Britain* (Dublin, 1732).
5 Joseph Addison, *Cato. A Tragedy* (1713), 2.1.
6 "To those whom God hath formed to another way of thinking, who have confined their ideas of merit, to loyalty, learning, religion, &c. duty, is honour,–and the solid joys of a good conscience, solid glory!" Delany, *Revelation Examined*, vol. 2, xxi.
7 Phillips's reference to writing "the whole Duty of Woman" alludes to an anonymous conduct and cookery book *The Whole Duty of a Woman*, published earlier in the century, itself an allusion to Richard Allestree's *The Whole Duty of Man*.
8 Thomas Sherlock, *The Use and Intent of Prophecy, in the Several Ages of the World* (London, 1732), 53. Sherlock's text ends with "the Promise of God."
9 François de Salignac de la Mothe-Fénelon's *Les Aventures de Télémaque* (1699) was translated into English and published the same year. The work proved one of the most popular and influential books throughout Europe in the eighteenth century. Archbishop Tillotson's sermons were widely admired for their prose style and recommended as models for the clergy.
10 Prov. 12:4. "A virtuous woman *is* a crown to her husband: but she that maketh ashamed *is* as rottenness in his bones."
11 In her *Apology* Phillips refers to one of her lovers, Philip Southcote (1697/8–1758), as "Tartuff," evoking Moliere's play *Le Tartuffe, ou l'imposteur* (1669).
12 A number of the phrasings here echo Elizabeth Rowe's *Devout Exercises of the Heart: In Meditation and Soliloquy, Prayer and Praise*, first published in London, 1737.
13 Chapone's use of the phrase "inmost Recesses of the Mind" echoes a prefatory letter in the first edition of Samuel Richardson's *Pamela: or, Virtue Rewarded* (1740) attributed to William Webster, editor of the *Miscellany*.

Hardships of the English Laws – Appendices

Appendix One:
   Responses from the *Weekly Miscellany* (1736, 1737)

Appendix Two:
   Excerpts from *The Lawes Resolution of Womens Rights* (1632), *Baron and Feme: A Treatise of the Common Law. Concerning Husbands and Wives* (1700), and *The Treatise of Feme Coverts; or, The Lady's Law* (1732)

Appendix Three:
   Excerpts from the Sarah Chapone–Samuel Richardson correspondence, with passages from *The Hardships of the English Laws in Relation to Wives*

Appendix One
Responses from the *Weekly Miscellany* (1736, 1737)[1]

Following the publication of *The Hardships of the English Laws in Relation to Wives* in May 1735, portions were published in the May and June issues of the *Gentleman's Magazine*. There was little further response until the following year when a lengthy attack appeared in the *Weekly Miscellany* October 23, 1736, an excerpt of which was reprinted in the *Gentleman's Magazine* vol. 6, November 1736. The original letter prompted a second response published in the *Weekly Miscellany* a few weeks later. This second letter rejects completely Chapone's attempts to claim a biblical defence of her argument, and indulges in a jocular account of a battle of the sexes modeled on in Alexander Pope's mock-heroic poem *The Rape of the Lock*.

The following summer the editor of the *Weekly Miscellany* opened the August 19 issue with an admission that he has occasionally published letters purporting to be "by a Lady" that were in fact written by himself. The editor, writing under the name of "Richard Hooker, of the Temple," was the Rev. William Webster, described by Emily Lorraine de Montluzin as "a High-Church divine" who "established the paper's rabidly anti-Dissenter, anti-Methodist, and anti-Catholic character, dedicating the *Weekly Miscellany* so exclusively to religious and moral topics that it came to be known as 'Old Mother Hooker's Journal.'"[2] He assures his readers however that the letter that follows is genuinely the work of a woman writer, and for the benefit of his readers he has included his letter to her that prompted her reply. He explains that, on learning from a friend that a woman had written *The Hardships of the English Laws in Relation to Wives*, he sent via his friend copies of the letters about her pamphlet he had published the previous year. On receiving her reply, he appealed through the mutual friend for her permission to publish it, and, receiving no express denial, he is now publishing both his own letter and her response. In his letter he offers her the compliment of an invitation to contribute to the *Miscellany,* in particular to write on the concerns facing young women as they approach marriage, "by way of a supplement to Lord Hallifax's [sic] Advice to a Daughter."[3] Chapone must have been flattered by the invitation, perhaps seeing it as a gesture of reconciliation following the earlier critical responses. She acknowledges that she had read the earlier letters but claims she did not have time to reply to them (her allusion to their style of "Ridicule" suggests their sting), and although she appreciates his praise, she accuses him of misrepresenting her sentiments. She declines the offer, explaining that duties to her husband and family leave her no time to write. One wonders if her authorship of a work on the law might have become known beyond the Cotswold circle, and her heterodox views seen as incompatible with her position as a clergyman's wife. Her acquiescing to the publication of her refusal could be read as a public assertion of her familial and domestic priorities, hinting at the possibility even of a public recanting, while her criticisms that he misrepresented her arguments anticipate the resistance she will later offer to Samuel Richardson.

1 *Weekly Miscellany*, No. 300, Saturday, October 23, 1736

To Richard Hooker, *Esq*;

Sir,

In a mix'd Company the Discourses turn'd upon the odd Jumble of *Petitions* last Session, from *Jails* and *Universities*, *Conventicles* and *Cathedrals*, *Watermen*, *Quakers* and *Parsons*; when a *Lady* produced and read a Piece, intitled, The *Hardships of the* English *Laws relating to Wives, in an humble Address to the Legislature*. The Thing appear'd new and entertaining, and we could not help running out in Imagination, and fansying we saw all the good Wives of the Kingdom, with the Ladies of the Members of both Houses at their Head, marching in Procession to *Westminster*, their Eyes sparkling, Cheeks glowing, Lips moving, Pace quickening, and their Address waving in the Way of Banner before them: Nay, we went so far as to think we heard the universal Crack of Fans let off, upon being told the Petition was order'd to Lie upon the Table.[4]

I take the Author of this Pamphlet to be a great *Beauty*, from the Briskness of Stile, and assuming Air of the whole Performance, and am glad she did not prefix her Effigies before her work: One may talk *of* her, but it would be impossible to talk *to* and *against* her. However, instead of her *Picture*, she has given us her *Sex*, and the Inclinations of it, in the first Leaf of her Book, where she talks of heaping up Words, and shaking her Head at us; she might have added clapping her Hands too; since none of these Ways of Address have ever been denied to belong to those she is contending for. She explains herself further in her last Motto but one, where she calls Man her *Equal*: and *P. 55*. she founds all Authority in the marry'd State on *Superiority of Reason*, and laments for herself and Sex the Loss of the Advantages of Universities, publick Negotiations, and free Converse with Men; well knowing that a fine Woman was never in the wrong in an Argument in her whole Life, and that upon this Foot the Empire of the Sex would be as extensive as their Charms; and that the natural Knack of Disputation, improv'd by Schools, Universities, &c., would soon carry the Point for those Females, who had fewer Advantages of Person.

But now, in the Openness of my Heart, I cannot help acquainting my fair Adversary, for her Comfort, that I hear there is a Project on foot for introducing the *Female* World into all the Advantages of Education, by allowing the Fellows of Colleges to marry.[5] By this means the Academical Exercises will be considerably improved, Letters will be common to both Parties, and there will be no Houshold Cares (all being provided there by Men at a common Table) to hinder the Ladies from improving their Talents of Discourse, either in Publick Respondencies and Oppositions to other Peoples Husbands, or Private ones at home with their own. This may be a Door to all the other Employments of Life, at present engross'd by the *Men*. Female Ambition will scarce stop at the first Ascent: From thence the Prospect will enlarge and they will be led to plead their own Cause first, and next those of other People, in our Courts of Justice: They will then easily justify the peculiar Advantages of their Sex above the other, in Negociations with all amorous or complaisant foreign Princes. The Pleasure of talking for half an Hour without Contradiction, in an elevated Situation, will certainly carry them up into the dictating *Pulpit*. Their Fitness for the Office can never be disputed; Handsomeness of Person, and Volubility of Tongue, are some of the first Qualifications of an Orator; and the Display of the Handkerchief, and the various Arts and Instruments of soft Perswasion, seem to be some of those Things, which (in the Words of the Writer quoted by this Author) *require the delicater Hand and nicer Management and Genius of the Woman*; and then turning a Distaff (as Hercules was made to do) or stirring a stiff Pudding, would be construed some of those many Things *which require the more robust and active Powers of the Man*.[6] It is true, St. *Paul* puts in his Bar to this Claim, and allows not a Woman to teach, but orders her to learn in private of her Husband: But then (as this Author well observes) Christianity is going down apace, and Deism making great Strides towards us, and in that Case we shall be in the Golden Age of a State of Nature, and then the Apostle's Authority will be as obsolete as the *English* Laws against Women, founded upon that Authority.

I do not pretend to answer the Work of this Female Addresser, but shall only offer a few scattering Remarks upon it. She opens her Book with presuming on her Liberty of addressing the Throne, as an *English* Subject; and hopes this inestimable Privilege is not confined to the Male Line. I think her Claim is just, and if her Grievances are real, she could not have address'd any where with surer Prospect of Success, than to His Majesty. But yet how the Gentlemen, she applies to, will take this Address of their Wives, which in its true Construction amounts to a modest Petition for changing Places with them, no Body can say. This is certain, that an Order of *Males*, most like the Petitioners in their Impotency, retired Life, and Length of Habit, were said by some to be *Seditious*, for making a Request to be continued in their Rights and Properties as *Englishmen* and *Subjects*.

But let us open this *Pandora*'s Box: The first Complaint that flies out (*P.* 6. *Case* 1.) is, That by the Confession of our Laws, Wedlock is a worse Condition that Slavery itself: because, forsooth, in a Dispute about the Validity of a Woman's Will, annull'd by a Second Marriage, the Civilians, in the Course of the Argument, unluckily compar'd Marriage to a State of *Captivity* among the *Romans*, and the Court would not allow it the Privilege of that; because it was not, like that, forced, but voluntary.[7] Now I cannot, for my Life, see, how any Judge can be blamed, for not confirming a Will made in the first Widowhood of a Female, never known to be of the same Mind two Hours together, after her being marry'd, and a Widow the second Time, and she had forgot it, or, at least, presum'd no one could imagine that to be her last Will, between which and her last a thousand contradictory ones must have intervened.

The Second Case (which, I think, the Author has produced to her Shame) is an Elopement of a Wife from her Husband. The *Latins* had once the Privilege of marrying with the *Romans*; after many Unions of this Sort, a Rupture happened between the two Nations. The *Latins* demanded their Daughters; Leave was given for as many to return home as would; not one stirr'd. Now see the *English* Wife in the Case before us: Words pass'd between her Spouse, as sometimes will happen; Madam fir'd, and said she had Relations and Houses to go to: In short, she not only threaten'd, but did; she march'd off, and being brought back, chose to die of Vexation, rather than do the least Service for her Husband.

The following Cases are an horrible Outcry about Confinements; and the Grievance is, that the *English* Husband has the Power of confining a gossiping Wife, and is not hang'd, tho' she, thro' Impatience, throws herself out of Window, and breaks the Neck, which nothing could bend.

But see, the brisk, pretty Creature goes on, and says, Marry'd Women here have no Property; when it is notorious, that *Property*, where there is any, may be secured to the Wife, and generally is, by the *English* Laws, and (such is the Conscience of the Petitioners) usually double to what she brings into a Family, whose Expence she trebles; besides Pin-Money for private Pleasures.[8] If Women are often *kiss'd* or *kick'd* out of those Previous Settlements (according to the Joke of one of our Judges) it shews the Weakness of the Sex, and how improper it is they should be trusted with the Interests of others, who cannot maintain their own. But, on the other Hand, there are not wanting Instances of Men's being wheedled or huff'd, and sometimes tired, if not beaten, into Measures very disadvantageous to themselves.

Another Complaint (*P.* 15.) is, That tho' the Right of the wedded Pair in each other's Persons is equal, yet the Wife cannot break this Contract, and sin with as much Indemnity as her Husband. I am downright asham'd of this, and (to turn her own Words elsewhere upon her) shall dismiss it with saying, *Lewd Women do not deserve this Privilege, and chaste ones would not desire it.*

But (*P.* 17.) You are to hear the tender Mamma blubbering, because she cannot spoil her Children all thro' their Life, as she generally does at the Beginning of it, but the Man can put them out of her Power, if he thinks it proper. Instinct, not planted in vain, she says, is common to both Parents, perhaps strongest in the weaker. Be it so: What then? The Question is about *Education*, for which Judgment, not Fondness, is the best Qualification. The fondest Mother, therefore, may be unfit for the Trust; and since Somebody must judge, why not the Man?

It is impossible to hold this Female *Proteus*, who is Water, Fire in an Instant, slips thro' your Fingers, or burns them. Tell her she is happier than a Wife in *Turkey*: The Husband there may kill his Wife, but it is otherwise here; there he may have a whole Seraglio, here one Man is allow'd but one Woman, agreeably to the Appointment of God and Nature; she turns the Blessing into a Curse, and had rather be one of the neglected Many belonging to the Grand Seignoir, where the Tyranny of the Husband will be shared, than the Bosom Wife of an *English* Gentleman, where she must bear it all herself. Not so the *Roman* Matron, who, being misinform'd (in order to conceal the true Business) that the Fathers were deliberating on a new Law to enable Husbands to have two Wives apiece, thought it a Grievance so sensible, as to summon all the Ladies in *Rome*, and besiege the Senate-house.[9] The Exemption of Women from several Pains and Penalties by our Laws, is made an Objection to them. This Favour is an Insult, and supposes Women mere Nothings, and votes them dead in Law. They shall suffer for Treason committed with their Husbands; this is a Grievance: They shall not suffer in some other Cases; this is a Grievance also. The Husband is alone liable to Imprisonment for Debt, even of his Wife's contracting, before or after Marriage, and for neither has any Remedy; his Estate shall pay her Debts, while her Jointure and Settlement are untouch'd, and out of the Question: Yet these are no Privileges; they are Affronts to the Sex. Mercy on me! What would the Woman have?[10]

But if we will not be huff'd, we are to be sham'd out of our ill-manner'd Laws relating to Wives, which are said to be harder than those of old *Rome*. If the Fact is true, a Question arises, Whether the Merits of the Sex, in both Nations, are equal? The *Romans* were generally just to Desert, and grew great by a Spirit of Emulation for the Common Good, raised by this Conduct among all Orders of People. The Marriage of the first *Roman* Ladies was Captivity with a Vengence: They were taken by a *Rape*; but when the Arms of their Fathers and Relations were opposed to their Husbands for their Deliverance, they generously stept between the angry Parties, and left no Passage for their Swords, but thro' their own Bodies. Could Men be too indulgent to such Wives? When the Exigencies of State requir'd it, they redeem'd their Country with the only Ornaments they had, a little Gold in their Ears; and instead of spending Hours at the Glass, in adjusting their Hair, cut it off to make Ropes for the Defence of the Capitol. They knew not for Centuries what it was to drink strong Liquors, and were so far from prostituting their Chastity, that every Invasion of it cost a Revolution of the Government. Can any one, after this, envy them their Funeral Orations, and rideing in Chariots, and other Honours and Privileges, or wonder, there was not an Instance of Divorce of such Wives for Hundreds of Years? Let the Females, pleaded for, come up to this Parallel of Virtue and Publick Spirit, and then let them lay their Claim to equal Honours, and we will willing allow it. When the *English* History supplies us with an Instance of the Sacrifice of one Female Vanity to the Publick Good; if our Women will give up their Ornaments to the Exigence of the State, or, at least, avoid Dressing to the Ruin and Destruction of it: When they cover their Heads with Ten Pounds instead of an Hundred, in case of a common Calamity, and cease to sink the Joy of their Nuptials with an Expence, which often ruins a Family: When the Publick and Private Peace are their first Ambition: When we no longer see the Woods of an ancient Estate rooted up to glitter in Pebbles round a Neck which is far handsomer without that Collar, nor the Provision for half a Dozen Children thrown away for the Amusement of the fond Mother of them: We will then acknowledge the Justice and Politeness of the *Romans* to exceed and shame ours, as much as our Female Virtue, at present, falls short of theirs.

I have really so great an Esteem for the Good Sense and Wit of the Lady I have had some Words with, and such a Regard for her Interests, and those of her Sex, that I cannot close this Subject, without offering some Queries to her Consideration, which may either prevent, delay, or temper the intended Petition.

1.   Whether it is proper to apply at all to the Legislature for the Reformation of the Men; and whether such Reformation, if begun with one Sex, may not end with the other? Whether, in short, they had not better compromise Matters between themselves, than call in a third Power, which may ruin both; and, under the Notion of amending the Matrimonial State, extinguish all the little Love still subsisting between the marry'd Parties?

2.   Whether, in Case of an Application, the Complainants have their Proofs ready; for it is probable their bare Words will not be taken on this Occasion; since the Parliament have been so lately abused by a Sett of Men, who pretending to 1100 and odd Instances of Grievances, could nevertheless make out but two of this formidable Number.

3.   Whether Complaints from all the Wives in *England* may not be construed Petit-Treason? Whether, therefore, the same Thing may not be brought about more silently and effectually, if the Wives of the Clergy only appear upon this Occasion? It is evident, there never was a luckier Time for making Complaints against this Sett of Men; and it is equally evident, their Wives are under harder Provisions than others, and therefore may hope to come in for a Share of their Husbands Titles and Fortunes, whenever they come to be divided: And what, probably, may be granted in this Crisis to one Sett of Wives, may pave the Way for a general Law in Favour of the whole Sex, laboring under the present Disadvantages of Matrimony.

4.   Whether, upon the Whole, and the Uncertainty of the Issue, in any Application of this Sort, it may not be adviseable to defer an Address for bounding the Power of *English* Husbands, till they are found grosily to abuse it; which is not allow'd to be the present Case, by the Confession of the Complainants themselves. It is true, it may be said, the proper Season for applying for Laws against bad Husbands, is in the Time of good ones; as the best Provisions against Tyranny have always been made in the Reign of Princes, who were above exercising it. This, indeed, is a Compliment: But I will venture to say, when the Grievances are real and pressing, such Petition will be offer'd with more Spirit and a better Grace, and will obtain Redress from the governing Sex, or occasion a Revolution in it, as is usual in such Cases: And in the Battle of the Sexes, every one knows where the Odds will lie.

5. Whether in the mean Time, for the Convenience of the Ordinary People, there may not be erected, in Imitation of the States of *Holland,* a *Forbettering House,* (as it is called) whither, upon proper Application, the delinquent Party may be sent, and not be released thence, till it appears he or she has no further Occasion for such House. By this wise Contrivance the Children will not starve, or run out at Heels by the Negligence or Wilfulness of either Parent.

Yours, &c.

X.

2 *Weekly Miscellany*, No. 303, Saturday, November 13, 1736

To Richard Hooker, *Esq*;

The Letter in your *Miscellany*, on the *Hardships of the* English *Laws relating to Wives*, led me to buy the Pamphlet which occasion'd it. The ingenious Author, I believe, wrote most Part of her Piece for her own Diversion as well as ours, but at the latter End grows serious and seems to be in earnest, when she maintains the *original Equality of the Sexes*, and supports her Opinion by the Authority of *Hobbes*, Mr. *Wollaston*, and the Author of *Revelation examined with Candour*. What Verdict unassisted *Reason* would give in this Point I will not take upon me to say; but *Revelation* is clear on the other Side of the Question, and asserts the inferiority of Woman before, as well as confirms it after the Fall. According to the *Scripture* Account of these Things, Man was created first, and invested with Dominon over the Earth and its Inhabitants: Woman was soon after made, out of Man, for the Foundation of mutual Union and Endearment; but out of an inferior Part of him, perhaps, to intimate some Degree of Subordination. The End of her Formation was to be a Help-meet to Man, for his Convenience, Solace, Converse, and Use; but he, for whom this Companion was made, seems intended for the principal Figure of the Piece. These two Arguments are not barely conjectural, but authoritative and concluding; because they are adopted by the Apostle to the *Corinthians*, where he says, *That the Head of the Woman is the Man*, who by Virtue of his Superiority, should have his upper Part uncover'd, while a Covering, or Veil, should declare the Inferiority of the Female: His Reasons for this Pre-eminence of one Sex about the other, are, That *the Man is not of the Woman, but the Woman of the Man: Neither was the Man created for the Woman, but the Woman for the Man.* Accordingly, the Image of God, which contains in it Sovereignty, is apply'd to the Man alone, in the Text of *Genesis*, which says, *God created Man* (or rather, the Man) *in the Image of God created he him: Male and Female created he them.* This Passage St. *Paul* explains undeniably to this Sense, where he says, *Man is the Image and Glory of God, but the Woman is the Glory of the Man.*[11] He is the upper-most Creature of this sublunary World, and receiv'd immediately from his

Maker a Power to govern it: She, as made after, out of, and for him, is one Remove farther from the Fountain of Authority; she is the Image of God, only as she is the Image of her Husband. He is the Original, she is the Copy: He acts by his own inherent Right, she by a Communication of it, delegated from him, and in Subservience to him.

Full of this Thought, and a thousand others, which had crowded in upon this Occasion, I fell into a Sleep in my Chair, and was immediately transported into the Regions of *Fancy*. I saw all the Individuals of both Sexes, on a large Plain, very busy and eager in settling a Point which seem'd to be of the utmost Concern to them. I was very attentive to the Result, when on a sudden the Air trembled with the distant Sounds of Trumpets, which grew stronger as they approach'd nearer to the Centre of this vast Assembly, and were follow'd by an *Herald*, who, with a Voice reaching the utmost Boundaries of the Place, pronounc'd, It was decreed by MAN, the Lord of this Creation, *That from henceforth the Wife shall depend upon her Husband in all Matters of Pleasure, Diversion and Delight; her Desires shall be circumscribed by his, whom she shall reverence in Acquiescence to Divine Authority; he shall have the Supreme Command in his Family, and she shall act in Subordination to him.* The Declaration ended, confused Murmurs arose, succeeded by triumphant Songs and Shrieks, which pierced the skies. At the Instant the Women disengag'd themselves from those of the other Sex, and, filing off, form'd themselves into two Lines: One, consisting of those who were faulty in Shape, Complexion, or Feature, under two Leaders; *Scorn*, pale as Death, and *Passion*, in a Flame-colour'd Habit, with such Arms as Fury ministred, Stones and Dirt from the Ground, and Revilings from an inexhaustible Storehouse within themselves; the other, made up of the choicest Beauties, the finest Shapes, the loveliest Skins, in the Bloom of Youth, and all the Elements of Attire, but with no Arms that were visible, under two other Commanders, *Pride* bearing an erect Plume of Peacocks Feathers, and *Cunning*, in a Dress of as many Colours as the Rainbow. It was judg'd shameful for all the Males at once to advance against this impotent Corps: The Soldiery, whose Business was fighting, were order'd to quell the Mutiny and bring the Deserters to Reason, or come to Extremities with them. But as the Affair was delicate, the sprucest and best bred Officers were chosen to conduct it, who pick'd out a Body of the neatest and handsomest Fellows in the Army, their Hair pasted and confined by bent Combs, and their Breasts adorned with ruffled Linnen, because these might be best spared, if they should suffer in the Action, and because they had the greatest Experience of this Sort of Enemies, and boasted many Victories over them. They advanced with the prettiest Step and Air imaginable, and presented their Bayonets screwed to the End of their Muskets. At a Signal, the first Female Line, after a Volley, retreated thro' the Space left for them behind the second, which advanced into its place, in all the Glare of Jewels, and Insolence of conscious Beauty. Their crested Heroine sprung a Pace forward, and addressing the Opposers, said, Is this your mighty Courage, Wisdom and Justice, to level your Arms against those who have none, to make up in brutal Force what you want in Reason, and murder those you have too long injur'd? O prodigious Heroes, where there is no Danger! Our Chains you have often worn; but we will never stoop to put on yours. Then, turning to the Ladies behind her, she said, Bare your Bosoms, and shew how much greater you are in meeting Death, than they in giving it.[12] The Command was no sooner given, than every Handkerchief flew off, and, at the same Instant, fiery Arrows, before undiscover'd, shot from their Eyes, and enter'd under the left Pap of every one in the opposite Line: They dropt their Pieces, and were approaching to surrender at Discretion, when a Retreat was sounded on both Sides, and a Parley agreed to; the Issue of which was, That the momentous Cause shou'd be argued by the Gentlemen of the *Long Robe*, and the *Lawyers* were order'd to prepare themselves accordingly.

A Superb Building, capacious enough to embrace this vast Multitude, rose up in a Moment, at the Direction of a Female Architect, in the Interest of her Sex, named *Imagination*. The Men were rang'd on one Side, and the Women on the other. The Walls were so polish'd, that by the Help of Lights properly disposed, the Ladies were not only seen in Front, but their Persons and Actions danced before the Eye, in every possible Direction of it: and the Situation of the Parts of the Structure was such, as to catch a Voice of a Female Pitch, and multiply it a thousand Times, and convey it to a thousand different Points. Above was a spacious Dome, in which, half folded within a Sable Cloud, sat *Judgment*, a bearded Figure, like *Homer's Jupiter* (but imagined to be of either Sex) looking down on the Assembly, of which he was appointed Arbitrator by both Sides, with *Truth* on his Right Hand, and *Love* on his Left, by Way of Assessors.

The Affair began with a Proclamation for Silence, which was but ill observ'd on one Side of the Hall. The Direction of the Court was desir'd, as to which Sex shou'd begin the Debate, who determin'd for the *Men*, and said, Since it was probable the *Ladies* would claim their Privilege of having the *last Word*, it was unreasonable they should insist upon having the *first* too. Upon this a *Young Barrister* rose, but appear'd in the utmost Confusion, and hesitated every Word he spoke; his Hand cou'd not hold his Papers still, nor his Voice utter the Contents of them; his Eyes, where-ever turn'd, met with something that diverted him from his Purpose. With much Difficulty, at last, he made a shift to name the Parties concern'd, the Nature of the Cause, and the Issue he hoped. He was supported by an *Old Serjeant*, who rais'd himself heavily from his Seat, and, putting on his Spectacles, said, He cou'd not help observing what Disadvantages all his Brethren, who cou'd see, labour'd under: That the Gentleman who open'd the Cause was never known before to stammer in his Speech or be at a Loss which Way to look – but thus it always was in Commerce with that insidious Sex, who by a Sort of Fascination robb'd Men of their Understandings and Senses: Thus they had just now foil'd the *Soldiery*, and were going to play the same Game over again here. That he was heartily sorry the Act against *Witches* was repeal'd, otherwise he should have moved for prosecuting them upon that Statute.[13] Among the *Egyptians*, he said, from a golden Chain round the Neck of the Supreme Justiciary hung a

Figure without Sight, the Emblem of Truth; and the Hieroglyphical Statue of a Judge was made without Hands, and with Eyes fix'd on the Ground; he wish'd something like it could be done in the present Case: He profess'd he did not speak on his own Account, who could not see half way cross the Hall; but for the Benefit of others concern'd with him, he moved, that the Lights might be extinguish'd, and the whole Affair be transacted in the Dark. An Outcry arose from the opposite Side, on this Occasion, and the Motion was represented as a Design of foul Play. Chicane and Knavery want the Veil of Secrecy and Concealment, but they had too nice a Regard for Virtue and Decency, to trust themselves among such Company, set loose from the Restraint of Publick Observation. Quiet being restor'd, the *Coif'd Advocate* proceeded with saying, he should trouble them with few Words, of which they would have enough, he doubted not, from another Quarter:[14] The Sovereignty in question was of the utmost Importance, and enjoy'd by one Party and aimed at by the other, from the Beginning of Time: This he undertook to prove by various Quotations from Civilians and common Lawyers, and Historians, and Records of every Age and Country; and that the Foundation of this acknowledg'd Pre-eminence could be no other than the superior Talents of the Possessors. Since then the present Situation of Things was agreeable to Reason and Law, he humbly beg'd Leave to presume, the Court wou'd expect strong Arguments, before it consented to eject his Clients from Rights so equitably acquir'd, and so long enjoy'd.

A beautiful young Matron, who had express'd Impatience several times while the Serjeant was speaking, took the Advantage of a Fit of Coughing the old Pleader fell into, and rising said, If it had not been for this Accident their Adversaries would have had the *first Word* and the *last* too, by leaving no Room for any Body else to speak at all. The Shrillness of her Voice awaken'd a nimble Female, unperceiv'd before, by Name *Eccho*, who mimick'd her Words, and the Titter of her Acquaintance, and sliding along from Wall to Wall, repeated them to every part of the Audience. Delighted with this fortunate Beginning, and conscious of the Attractions of her Person and Action, she insinuated to the Court, that if her Cause was not the clearest in the World, it had never been intrusted to so inexperienc'd and young a Manager, Stranger to Schools and Universities, and the Improvements of Education; Arms their Adversaries were afraid to put into their Hands, lest they, who were their Equals without them, shou'd be their Superiors with them. The Laws, said she, I own, are in Favour of the Men; but it is no Wonder, since the Men made them. But what signify Laws, which have never been *receiv'd* or *obey'd* by those whom they concern? The Prescription of *antiquated Statues* is, indeed, on the Side of the Males, but the Prescription of *Facts*, is on the Side of the Females, who have really govern'd the Men ever since there were any. I wish the Gentleman, who mention'd them, had given a Catalogue of those overbearing Talents, which give the Men Pre eminence, and demand Respect. If *Strength* is of the Number, the Horse is stronger than his Rider; if that noble Creature is yet inferior, because the other sits on him, so was *Socrates* to *Xantippe*, when he submitted to carry her.[15] If their *Strength* be allow'd greater, it will afford no great Compliment to their *Courage*, as appears from the late Action with the *Flower* of their Troops. History represents *Semiramis* equal to *Alexander*, and *Tomyris* was superior to *Cyrus*, whose Head she cut off, and sated with Blood. *Dido* founded as flourishing an Empire as *Romulus*, and the present *Czarina* is a better Soldier than the *Great Turk*.[16] *Queen Elizabeth* exceeded all the *Kings of England* in *Policy*; *Queen Anne* beat the *French*, and sav'd the Liberties of *Europe*. An *English* Author, call'd *Plutarch*'s Morals, has collected the Virtues and Exploits of Women, more in Number, and greater in Kind than ever were ascribed to the other Sex, by their own flattering Panegyrists.[17] As to *Wisdom*, the usual insolent Boast of the Men, what have they to support it? There have been, indeed, a few amongst them able to direct others, call'd, for this Reason, *Sophists* and *Philosophers*: But to allow these to be as wise as they pretended to be, is to confess the Generality of Men are not so. These Men would not be distinguish'd for their Understanding, if the rest were not notoriously deficient. If an Ability to direct others denominates a Person *wise*, Women in general have a Right to the Title, since the *weakest* of them direct the *most knowing* Husbands. *Themistocles* was growing vain of his Accomplishments and Address, which enabled him to govern *Greece*, by virtue of his ruling *Athens*, the commanding City of it, till he remember'd his Wife had a Title to higher Glory, since she govern'd *Him*. That Woman was designed for Empire, is plain from the Beauty of her Person: This is alone the Case of the human Species, the Males of all other Sorts of Animals being the finest Creatures. They who were intended by Nature to rule the World, were furnish'd with Charms to engage a willing Obedience; and that their Power might be unquestion'd and lasting, Submission to it was made delightful.

The Female Orator was going on with ceaseless Fluency, when she was interrupted by a Motion, made from the other Side of the Hall, and agreed to by the Court, that the *Clergy* might be permitted to use their Endeavours with the Ladies, who might, possibly, pay some Regard to *their* Laws, tho' they despised all *human* Constitutions and Authorities. The Order was going to be obey'd, and the Clerk was directed to read the Passages out of the Sacred Books, upon which those Gentlemen intended to proceed: But the triumphant unweary'd Pleader, taking a higher Tone of Voice, resumed the Discourse, and said, Those she spoke for, wou'd not allow themselves to be *preach'd*, any more than *beaten* or *pleaded* out of their Natural Rights: That this was a State-Affair, and their Reverences had nothing to do with it. The Question was no less, than which half of the Species should govern the other, and no wonder the *Parsons* were forward to meddle in it, whose Practice it had been to set up and depose Sovereigns, tread on the Necks of Emperors, and dispose of Crowns like Rattles. It was absurd to suppose, they could have any Weight with *her* Sex, who had so little among *their own*. For she had learn'd from the finest Writers among the Moderns, that these grave Persons first imposed Slavery on Mankind, and were Authors of all the Mischiefs in the World: That it was a poor Evasion, to distinguish between *Papists* and *Protestants*, those of one Age and Nation and those of another; since the *Poets* were allow'd to be inspired, and one of them had said,

—*Priests of all Religions were the same.*[18]

For her Part, she conceiv'd *Religion* was a Personal Thing, and one might make it, without Assistance, what one wou'd, and when one wou'd, as easily as a *Pincushion*. She not only objected to the Men, but their *Records* too, which she had been taught by the Adversaries themselves to suspect and disregard. If all other Difficulties could be removed, there still remain'd, in her Opinion an insuperable Objection to them, which was the Account they gave of the Origin of Woman: As soon might the finest China be made out of the coarsest Earthen Ware, as the delicate Complexions on one Side the Hall from the tawny Sides of those on the other. It was more rational as well as decent, to think, when *Venus* rose from the Ocean, her Daughters floated after her on Shells, white as their Faces. How beautiful and just was the Plan of *Pagan Theology*, which made the *Graces* and the *Muses* of the finer Sex, and exhibited *Apollo*, the Deity of Letters and Politeness, without a Beard? That the Sexes could never be cast in the same coarse Mould, was evident from the Confession of the Opponents themselves who, tho' under another System of Belief, yet in their Addresses to Women, allow them to have something celestial and above human. Heaven is in their Eyes and Arms, and Life and Death in their Smiles and Frowns; Adoration belongs to them, as Superior Beings, and to lie at their Feet is the Top of Men's Ambition.

Eccho was almost tired of her Office, when an End was put to her incessant Labours, by the Appearance of a golden Balance let down from above, on which were put the Merits of the litigating Parties: One Scale subsided, the other kick'd the Beam.[19] At that Instant, *Truth* recev'd an Imperial Crown from the Hand of the presiding Power, with Orders to place it on the Head of the Conquerors: *Love,* also, receiv'd a Circle of Flowers, gather'd from the Bowers of Delight, blooming with Youth, glowing with Desire, soft as Perswasion, and gay as Smiles, emitting Fragrance, and diffusing Pleasure; his Instructions were to fix it round the Temples of the Vanquish'd. A Declaration issued from the Throne, That the Sex to be crown'd, shou'd have the Right of Sovereignty; but the Sex whose Lot was the Wreath, shou'd certainly exercise it. The two Assessors put themselves on the Wing to execute their Commission, and *Truth* began to descend with the Ensign of Majesty: The Female Part of the Assembly started and turn'd away at his Appearance; either unable to bear the piercing Lustre of his Eye, or unwilling to stare on a naked Figure. As the two Messengers came nearer, floating in Air, with the Fates of the Sexes waving in their Hands, the Attention, and the Silence upon it was so great, that I waked for Want of that continued Sound, which had hitherto lengthen'd out my Slumber, and lost, with Regret, the Decision of this important Affair.

Yours, &c.
W.

3 *Weekly Miscellany*, No. 243, Friday, August 19, 1737

To the Lady who wrote the Hardships of the *English* Laws in Relation to Wives.

Madam,

I sent you two Letters publish'd in the *Weekly Miscellany* upon your Ingenious Book relating to *The Hardships of the* English *Laws concerning Wives* [sic], and now I take the Liberty of writing to you myself; tho' I know no more to *whom* I am writing than *you* know my real Name, Character, or Circumstances. Our Correspondence is something like a Conversation in *Masquerade*, but enter'd into with more innocent Intentions, and carried on with more Modesty than those Nocturnal Dialogues are. I cannot but look upon the *Advocate* for your Sex, and *'Squire Hooker*, as two Persons so very extraordinary in our way, we ought to be better acquainted. In an Age when so little Pains is taken to improve the Understandings of the Women, and so much Pains is taken to corrupt the Morals and Principles of the Men, a Lady that is capable of writing with great Strength and Perspicuity, and a Gentleman that believes his Religion, and has Zeal enough to defend it, are very great Curiosities in their kind. But as you, Madam, have shewn what the *Fair Sex* can do, whenever they think fit to exercise the fine Talents which Nature has given them, I hope *my* Example will have some Effect towards making the *'Squires* less ashamed of appearing in Defence of their Faith. Be that as it will, I am determin'd to *persevere*; and I dare be positive that, if you would come into my Assistance, the Undertaking will no longer be thought Romantic, nor the Execution of it below the Notice of the smartest Fellows about Town. The Design of the *Miscellany* is as extensive as *Your Genius* seems to be; and it will be almost as difficult for you to think of any Subject that will not be proper for the Paper, as to write any thing that will not be an Ornament to it: But, as more Public Matters will permit, I have an Intention to publish several Letters for the particular Service of the *Ladies*, upon very useful and new Subjects; such as the Behaviour of *single* Ladies to *Gentleman*; particularly to a Gentleman that makes his Addresses; concerning the Choice of a Husband, &c. by way of Supplement to *Lord Hallifax's Advice to a Daughter* [sic]. That judicious Writer has given excellent Directions, but has omitted them where they are most wanted; when your Sex are in the most *critical* Circumstances, before their Judgment comes to Maturity, or they have gain'd any Experience. Thro' the Ignorance of some Parents and the Neglect of others, many innocent Creatures come into a vicious, designing World, so utterly unacquainted with it, and so much at a loss to know how to conduct themselves in it, that, let their natural Modesty and good Sense be ever so great, they must often be guilty of *Improprieties*, and be drawn in to *Inconveniencies*, if not betray'd into *Vices*. And as to the most important Article of their whole Life, and what will have a great Influence on their *future* Welfare, I mean, the *Choice of a Husband*; Parents generally have as little considered it, and judge as ill of it, as the Children can do. The *Authority* of *Parents* in the Disposition of their Children in *Marriage*, and the Direction of them in their Behaviour towards their *Lovers*, has been very greatly abused, for the Gratification of a tyrannical or avaricious

Temper, and to the Corruption of the most innocent Minds in their Notions of *Sincerity* and *Honour* in Matters that require an Observance of the strictest and nicest Rules.[20] These Points, Madam, will require the Acuteness of your Observations, and the Delicacy of your Pen; and you must excuse my Freedom if I tell you, that, if you refuse *Religion* and *Virtue* the Benefit of your uncommon Abilities when they stand so much in need of your Help, I shall suspect your *Faith* as much as I admire your *Parts*; but in better Hopes I beg Leave to subscribe myself,

> *Madam,*
> *Your most Obedient,*
> *Though unknown,*
> *Humble Servant,*
> *From the Temple,*
> R. Hooker.

April 23, 1737.

To Richard Hooker, *Esq;*

April the 28th, 1737.

Sir,

I had the Honour of a Letter from you last Post, together with a printed *Address to the Ladies in general.* Your Letter was written with so much good Sense, and with such an Air and Spirit of Candour and Piety, that how unworthy soever I may think myself of the Honour done me in it, I neither dare impeach the Abilities, nor Integrity of the Author, by rejecting any Part of his praise, which like the signal Blessings of GOD, upon some of my Actions, humbles me under a Sense of unmerited Favours.

This, Sir, is my Sense of the Complimental Part of your Letter, what next falls under my Consideration, is the Matter of it. The Subjects you propose to write upon are of the highest Importance to the Community in general, and may be of particular Service to our Sex. But, alas! Sir, We are so sunk in Ignorance and Folly, that I know not who will be able to extricate us out of those Mazes of Impertinence, in which your Sex have involved us! You tell us (and we are bound upon our Allegiance to believe you) That the very *End* of our Creation was for your *Service* and *Delight.*—That our utmost Honour consists in your Approbation,—our highest Advancement in becoming your *Subjects,*—and our Truest Wisdom in submitting to your *Direction.* The Law gives us no Authority to *act,* and Custom, the greater Tyrant of the two, prohibits our *thinking* for ourselves. We never can rise above our first Principle, nor be rated higher than our intrinsic Valuation. If therefore we were created *merely* for you, 'tis enough if we can look Prettily *before* and do as we are *Bidden after* Marriage. That our Sex have a strong Influence upon yours is founded in Nature, no Learning can evade, no Strength subdue their

Power. But this improper Treatment of the Sex has render'd it so ridiculous, that a Man is ashamed to acknowledge what he feels, or to be influenced by a Creature he has made so insignificant. To what End should you write to those who were never taught to *read*? I have once found it to little Purpose, and perhaps when you write you may find it to less, for,

— *Stars beyond a certain Height,*
Give Mortals neither Heat nor Light.[21]

There is such a mutual Relation, and close Connection, between Ignorance and Pride, that while Women are educated as they are at present, they will be fond of Flattery, and consequently prefer him, who has the greatest Skill in it. And so long as Men over-rate their Pretentions, and fancy themselves *superior Intelligences*, or in other Words, of a more *dignified Nature*, they never will qualify us to judge for ourselves, by allowing us a Rational Education. You see, Sir, that I take the Liberty to dissent from some of your Sentiments, in your ingenious Letters printed in your *Miscellany*, for which I beg Pardon, because I have not time at present to controvert them. Want of time indeed was the Reason why I took no Notice of those Letters, otherwise I should have made some Reply to them: though they were written in a Stile I should never chuse to engage in, having neither Inclinations to, nor Talents for Ridicule. However I was well entertained by them, and acknowledge they were Polite, and that you allowed me more than I could claim, as to my Abilities, though you allowed me less, as to my Arguments, and misrepresented my Sentiments.

After all, I would not be understood to disapprove or discourage you in your laudable Undertaking. I admire and honour you for it; and wish to GOD it were in my Power to assist you in it. After having assum'd the Confidence to publish my Thoughts, it might look like Affectation to say, That I questioned my Abilities, yet really I do, Sir, especially in my present Circumstances, which lay me under an Obligation to employ my Time in my own Family, which is a pretty large one, yet consists mostly of Children, with whom I spend six or eight Hours every Day. My Husband and I are both so apprehensive of the reigning Impiety of the Age, that we dare not trust our Children from us, and therefore educate them ourselves; I assist as far as I am capable, which, together with the necessary Affairs of the Family, engrosses all my Time. If I have any Merit, it is in cheerfully quitting my *Book* and my *Pen*, for the *Needle* and *Distaff*; and endeavouring to do my Duty in that humble State of Life in which it has pleased GOD to place me. Far from assuming the Province of Direction, I am sufficiently happy if I can make my slender Abilities of any use to my Husband, to whose generous Spirit I owe the Improvements of them, and who has therefore all imaginable Right to claim their Application to his Ease and Service. Were I disengaged from these Domestic Duties and Employments, I should with Joy embrace the happy Opportunity you kindly offer me, of improving my Understanding, and assisting your generous Endeavours for the Service of Mankind. No Proposal could be more agreeable to me. As we are utter Strangers to each other, we should be free from all those personal Prejudices, which are too apt to mix themselves in all our Researches after Truth; and to darken that natural Light of the Understanding, which, as far as it goes, *is* a sure Guide. For we cannot impute our Mistakes to any inbred Quality in the Intellect, because then false Judgments would be natural to it, and if so we never could be assured of any Truth, except this, That we must be always in Error.

After this plain artless Relation of my Circumstances, I hope Sir, that you will acquit me of the Charge of want of *Faith*, or Zeal for my Religion and Country, if I should continue to circumscribe my Inclinations, by not suffering them to carry me beyond Domestic Duties, till my Children shall no longer want my constant Care and Instruction. Whenever I can command a little Time, it shall be laid out as you require.

I pray GOD give you Success, with every solid Pleasure arising from Learning and Piety. I am, with great Acknowledgments for the Honour you have done me,

> *SIR,*
> *Your most Obedient*
> *Humble Servant.*

Notes

1 The *Weekly Miscellany*, 1736, 1737 (London, England). *17th–18th Century Burney Collection Newspapers*. Gale Cengage. All excerpts from the *Miscellany* are from this edition.

2 Emily Lorraine de Montluzin, *Attributions of Authorship in the* Gentleman's Magazine, *1731–1868: An Electronic Union List*. For Vol. 6 (1736), Charlottesville, Bibliographical Society of the University of Virginia, 2003. http://bsuva.org/bsuva/gm2/GMintro.html.

3 Lord Halifax's *The Ladies New-year's Gift; or, Advice to a Daughter*, first published in 1688, remained one of the most popular conduct books of the eighteenth century.

4 To be ordered to "lie upon the table" meant the petition was to be set aside, or ignored.

5 Fellows of Oxford and Cambridge Universities were not allowed to marry; this requirement remained in place until the nineteenth century.

6 The italicized passages are from William Wollaston, quoted by Chapone in *Hardships of the English Laws*. Hercules was sold as a slave to Omphale and required to spin wool, hence a figure of effeminacy and weakness.

7 In England, several areas of law including those of the church and the admiralty were based on Roman civil law, and lawyers who practiced in these fields of law were known as civilians.

8 See introduction p. 1–2 for discussion of jointures, portions, and pin-money.

9 Taken to the Roman Senate as a young man by his father, and unwilling to disclose its business to his mother, Papirius falsely told her that the Senate had proposed a law allowing a husband two wives.

10 One of numerous instances of the writer's deliberate misrepresentations of Chapone's words: for Chapone's discussion of the difficulties in determining a suitor's financial situation see p. 41–43.

11 For passages of St. Paul see 1 Cor. 11.3–9; for creation story see Gen. 1.27.

12 In Book One of Virgil's *Aeneid*, Penthesilea, queen of the Amazons, is described as wearing a gold band beneath her bared breast.

13 The laws against witchcraft in Great Britain were repealed in 1736.

14 The coif was a white cap worn over the wig by a sergeant-at-law at the Court of Common Pleas.

15 Socrates' wife Xanthippe was reputed to be a shrew and a scold, and one account has her demanding Socrates carry her on his back.

16 Anna Ivanova was Empress of Russia, 1730–1740.

17 Plutarch's *Moralia* included "The Virtues of Women," twenty-seven stories of courageous women; the reference here is unclear.

18 From John Dryden's *Absalom and Achitophel* (1681).

19 The reference to a golden scale is the most obvious of several allusions in this passage to Alexander Pope's *The Rape of the Lock* (1712, 1714), and an echo of his mock-heroic borrowings from the *Iliad* and the *Odyssey*.

20 These concerns will be taken up by Samuel Richardson in his novel *Clarissa* (1748–1749), and his circle of correspondents.

21 From Jonathan Swift, *Cadenus and Vanessa*.

Appendix Two

Excerpts from *The Lawes Resolution of Womens Rights* (1632), *Baron and Feme: A Treatise of the Common Law. Concerning Husbands and Wives* (1700), and *The Treatise of Feme Coverts; or, The Lady's Law* (1732)

Much of the common law in England that governed most aspects of women's lives —marriage, children, and inheritance—was shaped by centuries of land law, outlined in exhaustive detail in Sir Edward Coke's *The First Part of the Institutes of the Laws of England: or, A Commentary upon Littleton*, 1628.[1] A few years later the first book to address explicitly questions of women and the law appeared, *The Lawes Resolution of Womens Rights* (1632). A second work addressing primarily the laws of marriage, *Baron and Feme*, was published in 1700. Both were highly technical works designed for the practitioner (and relied heavily upon Coke), as was a subsequent work, *A Treatise of Feme Coverts* (1732).[2] Despite the latter's claim that "the Fair Sex" would learn "how to preserve their Lands, Goods, and most valuable Effects" it is doubtful that many women would have the legal expertise to benefit from it. Additionally, most law books still relied heavily on Latin and on law French (a mix of English and French dating from the Norman period), and would be relatively inaccessible to the uninitiated.

The feudal traditions that dominated the law of property in England up to the nineteenth century, especially real property, provided a unique status of *coverture* for married women, under which their civil being was suspended, or "covered" by the husband, and as *feme coverts* they were severely disabled in law, unable to own property or make contracts. (These points are discussed in Scott v. Manby 1663; see the report of Judge Hyde's ruling in *A Treatise of Feme Coverts* below.) The law both reflected, and reinscribed, the secondary status of women in Christian tradition; the excerpts that follow illustrate the merging of that legal and religious prescription. Chapone does not cite any of these works as sources and includes only works on the civil law (suggesting a reliance upon her husband and her brother Robert, both trained in civil law), making her own work on the law all the more remarkable.

The excerpts below from *The Lawes Resolutions* illustrate the enmeshing of civil and doctrinal prescription of women's lives. The passages from *Baron and Feme* outline the contemporary understanding of the concept of coverture and its impact on women and property. The ruling in the complex case of *Manby* v. *Scott* included in *A Treatise of Feme Coverts* reflects contemporary judicial fears of a wife's independent capacity to act. It addressed the question of contract at common law; the case for necessities also fell under the jurisdiction of the church. What is of interest here is the understanding of coverture implied by Justice Hyde's rationale. The case began in 1659 with a final ruling in 1663. The judges acknowledged that courts had earlier recognized a wife's capacity to bind her husband for the payment of necessities, a provision that also fell under the jurisdiction of the church, but a majority decision found that the common law did not recognize this power.[3]

1 The Lawes Resolutions of Womens Rights[4]

LIB.I. SECT. I

. . . though I bee unworthy to have the Marshalling of the titles of the Lawe to bring all matter cohering under them, yet I will make a little assay what I am able to doe if I were put to it in a popular kind of instruction: following a frame by distinction of persons, chasing the primary distribution of them made before the World was seven daies old, Masculum & Foeminam fecit eos, of which division because the part that wee say hath least judgement and discretion to bee a Law unto it selfe, (Women onely Women) they have nothing to do in constituting Lawes, or consenting to them, in interpreting of Lawes, or in hearing them interpreted at lectures, leets or charges, and yet they stand strictly tyed to mens establishments, little or nothing excused by ignorance, mee thinks it were pitty and impiety any longer to hold from them such Customes, Lawes, and Statutes, as are in a maner, proper, or principally belonging unto them: Laying aside therefore these titles which include onely the masculine, as Bishop, Abbot, Prior, Monke, Deane and Chapter, Viscount, Coroner, together with those which bee common to both kinds, as Hereticke, Traitour, Homicide, Felon, Laron, Paricide, Cutpurse, Rogue, with Feoffor, Feoffee, Donor, Donee, Vendor, Vendee, Recognisor, [3] Recognisee, &c. I will in this Treaty with as little tediousnesse as I can, handle that part of the English Lawe, which containeth the immunities, advantages, interests, and duties of women, not regarding so much to satisfie the deep learned or searchers for subtility, as woman kind, to whom I am a thankfull debter by nature (2–3).

LIB.I. SECT. III

The punishment of Adams sinne

Returne a little to Genesis, in the 3. Chap. whereof is declared our first parents transgression in eating the forbidden fruit: for which Adam, Eve, the serpent first, and lastly, the earth it selfe is cursed: and besides, the participation of Adams punishment, which was subjection to mortality, exiled from the garden of Eden, injoyned to labor, Eve because shee had helped to seduce her husband hath inflicted on her, an especiall bane. In sorrow shalt thou bring forth thy children, thy desires shall bee subject to thy husband, and he shall rule over thee.

See here the reason of that which I touched before, that Women have no voice in Parliament, They make no Lawes, they consent to none, they abrogate none. All of them are understood either married or to bee married and their desires or subject to their husband, I know no remedy though some women can shift it well enough. The common Law here shaketh hand with Divinitie, but because I am come too soone to the title of Baron and feme, and Adam and Eve were the first and last that were maried so young, it is best that I runne back againe to consider of the things (which I might seeme to have lost by the way) that are fit to be knowne concerning women before they be fit for marriage (6).

LIB.III. SECT. VIII

That which the Husband hath is his owne.

But the prerogative of the Husband is best discerned in his dominion over all externe things in which the wife by combination devesteth her selfe of proprietie in some sort, and casteth it upon her governour, for here practice every where agrees with the Theoricke of Law, and forcing necessity submits women to the affection thereof, whatsoever the Husband had before Coverture either in goods or lands, it is absolutely his owne, the wife hath therein no seisin[5] at all. If any thing when hee is married bee given him, hee taketh it by himselfe distinctly to himselfe.

If a man have right and title to enter into Lands, and the Tenant enfeoffe the Baron and Feme [the landholder puts the husband and wife into full possession of land], the wife taketh nothing. Dyer fol. 10. The very goods which a man giveth to his wife, are still his owne, her Chaine, her Bracelets, her Apparell, are all the Good-mans goods.

If a Woman taketh more Apparell when her husband dyeth then is necessarily for her degree, it makes her Executrix de son tort demesne, 33. H. 6. A wife how gallant soever she be, glittereth but in the riches of her hus- [130] band, as the Moone hath no light, but it is the Sunnes (129–130).

2 Baron and Feme: A Treatise of the Common Law. Concerning Husbands and Wives[6]

TO THE READER.

Having Methodized and Explained the Law concerning Infants, by a natural Chain of Thought, I was prompted to reflect upon the Law as it respects the Parents: And I had some Reason to conceive and hope, that a Treatise of this Nature (having been never hitherto designedly perused) might meet with an Entertainment agreeable. It is a Subject so copious that we shall find something or other relating to Baron and Feme in almost every Folio of our Law-Books, either in respect of Conveyances, Acts Judicial, Acts *in Pais*, Testaments, Actions or Pleadings, &c. All which I have here methodized, explained or corrected, as Occasion led me to it.

[A3v] I have herein considered *Baron and Feme* in all the Circumstances of Life, from the Solemnization of Marriage to the Divorce, and have not omitted those Collateral By-blows, (the Title of *Bastardy* making a considerable Figure in our Books;) and the Variety of the Matter made me some Attonement for the Labour.

I have been something tedious in considering what Alterations are made by the Intermarriage as to Estates, Leases, Chattels and Actions, and what Things of the Wife accrue to the Husband by the Intermarriage, or not; and what Acts, Charges or Forfeitures made or committed by the Husband, shall bind the Wife after his Death; as well knowing that they are of frequent Use, and consequently carefully to be examined.

But I have not been over-solicitous in Attornments, Disseisins, Remitters and Warranties, and such like, which have a Respect to real Actions concerning Feme Coverts; our Law having been much abridged and altered in such Cases, and our Settlements and Deeds of Trust as they are now framed, will strike off, and abate many of the Moot Cases; and whoever has a Mind to be curious about them, may with great Satisfaction consult the first Institutes, where they are largely and most excellently handled. However, [A4r] I have not totally omitted them, but have touched on some Cases which may be obvious in Practice, and by which an ingenious and well-disposed Student may improve his Notions, without heaping up other Cases or Points, one whereof perhaps may not be started in his Practice once in an Age. Only in the Section where and in what Cases *Baron and Feme* shall take by Interest or Moieties, I have been more exact, for that it is a curious and useful Learning.

As to what Acts or Contracts made by the Wife shall bind the Husband, the Resolutions of our Books have not been very consistent till that great Case (in point of Consequence) I mean of *Scott* and *Manby*, which was solemnly debated and settled in the *Exchequer-Chamber* by as learned Judges as every sate at one time in *Westminster-Hall*. Which long Arguments I have abridged and reduced to certain Propositions.

We likewise find our Books have been very wavering about *Baron and Feme's* Joinder in Action; but I have brought them into seven or eight Rules, by which a Studious Mind may easily be directed how to advise in such Cases.

And under every several Action brought by or against Husband and Wife, I have shewed the manner of declaring and Pleading under each Action, which makes the [A4v] Chapters of Declarations and Pleadings much shorter than they would have been.

As for the Faults herein committed, I have no Way but (*me ipsum tegere*) to shelter my self under the Coverture of your Candor and Ingenuity [A4ᵛ].

Chap. II. The Nature of a Feme covert

Coverture is *tegere* in *Latin*, and is so called for that the Wife is *sub potestate viri*.[7] The Law of Nature hath put her under the Obedience of her Husband, and hath submitted her Will to his, which the Law follows, *cui ipsa in vita sua contradicere non potuit*;[8] and therefore will not bind her by her Acts joining with her Husband, because they are judged his Acts, and not hers; she wants Free-will as Minors want Judgment; and yet the Law of the Land for Necessity-sake makes bold with this Law of Nature in a special kind, and therefore allows a Fine levied by the Husband and his Wife, because she is examined of her free Will judicially by an authentical person trusted by the Law, and by the King's Writ, and so taken in a sort as a sole Women; and also when she comes in by Receipt *Hob*. 225.

[8] A Feme covert in our Books is often compared to an Infant,[9] both being Persons disabled in the Law, but they differ much; an Infant is capable of doing any Act for his own Advantage, so is not a Feme Covert. A Lease made by an Infant without Rent is not void, but voidable; but it is void in the case of a Feme covert. If a Feme covert enter into Bond, *Non est factum* may be pleaded to it; but if an Infant enter into Bond, he must plead the special Matter, That he was under Age. An Infant may bind himself for Conveniencies, as Necessaries for himself and Family, and the Law giveth him Authority so to bind himself; but a Feme covert cannot do so without the Consent actual or implied of the Husband, because thereby she is to bind another that hath all the Property in her Estate, as was the Opinion of the Lord Chief Justice *Hale* in *Scot* and *Manby's* Case. And yet a Feme covert is a Favourite of the Law, and therefore the Law gives her *rationabile Estoveriam*, till Dower assigned: And it is said in some of our Book an Action lies not by the Executors against her for her *Paraphernalia* (7–8).

Chap. IX. Paraphernalia

By our Law the Apparel of the Wife is called *Bona Paraphernalia*. The Wife by the Common Law ought to have her necessary Apparel for her Body after the Death of the Husband, and not the Executors of the Husband; but she shall not have excessive Apparel.

If the Husband deliver to his Wife a Piece of Cloth to make a Garment and dies, albeit it was not made into a Garment in the Life of [73] the Husband, yet the Wife shall have it and not the Executor, inasmuch as it was delivered to her to that Intent. But against the Debtee of the Husband the Wife shall have no more Apparel than is convenient. *Mich*. 40 & 41 *Eliz. Harwel's* Case.

A Chain of Diamonds and Pearls being worth 370 *l*. being usually worn by a Woman who was the Daughter of an Earl in *Ireland*, and a Baron of *England*, and the Wife of a Knight and the King's Serjeant at Law, shall be *Bona Paraphernalia*; so that the Husband cannot devise them from the Wife. *Cro. Car.* 343. The Lord *Hastings* and *Dowglass. Richardson* and *Crook* thought the Wife shall not have them as *Bona Paraphernalia*, because they were not necessary for her, but only convenient: *Jones* and *Berkly e contra*: But all agreed she shall have her necessary Apparel (72–73).

Chap. XXI. Of Separate Dispositions

The Wife of an Improvident Husband had, unknown to him, by her Frugality, raised some Monies for the good of their Children, which she had disposed of for that Purpose being no otherwise provided for: this Disposition of the Wife the Lord Chancellor established by Decree; but afterwards upon Review and Assistance by the Judges, this Decree was reversed, as being dangerous to give a Feme Power to dispose of her Husband's Estate: This was *Scot* and *Brograve's* Case, *Anno* 1639. but in *George's* and *Chancey's* Case a Disposition by a Feme Covert of Money raised out of separate Maintenance, is good against the Husband (222).

3 The Treatise of Feme Coverts; or, The Lady's Law[10]

The Argument of JUDGE HIDE *in the Exchequer Chamber*, Term. Trin. 15. Car. 2. *in the Case of Manby and Scot, whether and in what Cases, the Husband is bound by the Contract of the Wife.*

A Feme Covert departs from her Husband against his Will, and continues absent from him divers Years; afterwards the Wife desires to Cohabit with her Husband, but he refuseth to admit her, and from that Time the Wife lives separate from him: During this Separation, the Husband forbids a Tradesman of *London* to Trust his Wife with any Goods or Wares; and yet for some Years before and afterwards he allows his Wife no Maintenance: The Tradesman contrary to the Prohibition of the Husband, sells and delivers Wares to the Wife upon Credit, at a reasonable Price; and the Wares so sold to the Wife are necessary for her, and suitable to the Degree of her Husband: The Wares are not paid for; wherefore the Tradesman brings an Action upon the Case against the Husband, and declares that the Husband was indebted to him in 40 *l.* for Wares and Merchandizes formerly to the Husband sold and deliver'd; and that the Husband in Consideration thereof, did promise to pay the said [178] Money: That the Husband hath not paid the same, tho' thereunto requir'd; and for that Money the Action is brought. Now, whether this Action will lie against the Husband for the Wares thus sold and delivered to the Wife, contrary to the Prohibition of the Husband, or not, is the Question?

This Case is the meanest that ever received Resolution in this Place; but as the same is now handled, it is of as great Consequence to all the King's People as any Case can be; it concerns every individual Person of both Sexes, that is, or hereafter shall be Married within this Kingdom, in the first and nearest Relation betwixt

Man and Wife: It toucheth the Man in point of his Power and Dominion over his Wife, and it concerns the Woman in point of her Substance and Livelihood; and I will deliver my Opinion plainly and freely, according as I conceive the Law to be, without favouring the one, or courting the other Sex.

First, I hold, that the Husband shall not be charged by such a Contract, tho' he do not allow any Maintenance to his Wife. *Secondly*, admit the Husband were chargeable generally by such a Contract; yet I conceive, that this Action doth not lie for the Plaintiff, as the Declaration is, and as the Verdict is found against the Defendant in this particular Case.

For the first, every Gift, Contract or Bargain, contains an Agreement on the Behalf of the Contractor or Bargainor, that the Donee or Bargainee shall have the Things contracted for; and the other is content to take them, and so in every Contract there is a mutual Assent of the Minds of the Parties, which mu- [179] tual Assent is an Agreement. *Plowd.* 17. *Fogasse's* Case. But a Feme Covert cannot give a mutual Assent of her Mind, nor do any Act without her Husband; for her Will and Mind (as also her self) is under and subject to the Will or Mind of her Husband; and consequently she cannot make any Bargain or Contract of her self, to bind her Husband.

In the Beginning when GOD created Woman an Help meet for Man, he said *They Two shall be one Flesh*; and thereupon our Law says, that Husband and Wife are but one Person in the Law: Presently after the Fall, the Judgement of GOD upon Woman was, *Thy Desire shall be to thy Husband, for thy Will shall be subject to thy Husband, and he shall Rule over Thee*. 3 Gen. 16. Hereupon our Law puts the Wife *Sub potestate viri*, and says, *Quod ipsa Potestatem sui non habeat, sed vir Suus*; and she is disabled to make any Grant, Contract or Bargain, without the Allowance or Consent of her Husband. *Bract. lib.* 3. *cap.* 32. 1 *Roll.* 351. *pl.* 45, 46. The Words of the Books and Authorities of our Law to prove this Point are observable; namely, if a Feme Covert make a Contract, or buy any Thing in the Market, or elsewhere, without the Consent of her Husband, tho' it come to the Use of the Husband, yet the Contract is void, and shall not charge the Husband; but if a Man command or Licence his Wife to by [sic] Things necessary, or Agree that she shall buy, he shall be bound by this Command or Licence. Old *Nat. Br.* 62. 21 *H.* 7. 70 *Fitz. N. B. R.* 120. Which proves, that it is not the Buying or Contract of the Wife, which Binds or Charges the Husband, [180] (for that is void in itself) but the Command or Licence of the Husband, which makes it the Contract or Bargain of the Husband.

As to my Brother *Twisden*'s Argument for the Woman's Power, when he says, that all those Books are where the Wife deals or trades as a Factor to her Husband, and all grounded upon that Reason, the Words themselves prove the Contrary; for the Difference taken by all the Books is, between the Buying and Contract of the Wife, without the Knowledge or Consent of her Husband; and a Buying or Contract had by the Wife, with Allowance or Command of the Husband. In the first

Case, the Buying or Contract is void; in the other, the Allowance or Command makes it good, as the Contract or Bargain of the Husband: Besides, weigh the Inconveniences which would follow, if the Law were otherwise.

Judges, in giving their Judgments and Resolutions in Cases depending before them, are to judge of Inconveniencies as Things illegal; and an Argument *ab inconvenienti* is very strong to prove that it is against Law. *Plowd.* 279. Then examine the Inconveniencies which must ensue, if the Law were according to my Brother *Twisden* and *Tyrrel's* Opinions: If the Contract or Bargain of the Wife, made without the Allowance or Consent of the Husband, shall bind him upon Pretence of necessary Apparel, it will be in the Power of the Wife (who by the Law of GOD and of the Land, is put under the Power of the Husband, and is bound to live in Subjection to him) to Rule over her Husband, [181] and undo him, and it shall not be in the Power of the Husband to prevent it. For here the Wife shall be her own Carver, and Judge of the Fitness of her Apparel, of the Time when it is necessary for her to have new Cloaths, and as often as she pleases, without asking the Advice or Allowance of her Husband: And will Wives depend on the Kindness and Favours of their Husbands, or be observant towards them as they ought to be, if such a Power be put into their Hands?

Then admitting, that the Wife in Truth wants necessary Apparel, and thereupon she goes into *Ludgate Street* to a Mercer and takes up Stuff, and makes a Contract for necessary Clothes; thence she goes into *Cheapside*, and takes up Linen there in like Manner; and also goes into a third Street, and fits herself with Ribbonds, and other Things suitable to her Occasions, and her Husband's Degree: This done she goes away, disposeth of the Commodities to furnish herself with Money to go Abroad to *Hide-Park*, or to Play at Gaming, or the like. Next Morning, this good Woman goes Abroad into some other Part of *London*, makes her Necessity and want of Apparel known, and takes more Wares upon Trust, as she had done the Day before; after the same Manner she goes to a third and fourth Place, and makes new Contracts for fresh Goods; none of these Tradesman knowing or imagining she was formerly furnish'd by the Others, and each of them seeing and believing her to have great need of the Commodities sold her; shall not the Husband be chargeable and liable to pay every one of [182] these, if the Contract of the Wife doth bind him? Certainly he is, and where this will End no Man can foresee (177–182).

Notes

1   Thomas Littleton's *Tenures* (1481 or 1482) outlined the basics of England's land law and was the standard reference until Coke's heavily glossed edition replaced it.

2   For facsimile editions of all three works including *The Hardships of the English Laws*, with a comprehensive introduction, see *Legal Treatises. Essential Works for the Study of Early Modern Women, Series III, Part One,* 3 vols, selected and introduced by Lynne A. Greenberg (Farnham, UK: Ashgate, 2005).

3   See A. W. B. Simpson, *A History of the Common Law of Contract: The Rise and Fall of the Action of Assumpsit* (Oxford: Clarendon Press, 1987), 545–557.

4   T[homas E[dgar], *The Lawes Resolutions of Womens Rights* (London 1632. Rpt. Amsterdam: Theatrum Orbis Terrarum; Norwood, NJ: Walter J. Johnson, 1979).

5   Seisin is "possession as of freehold," s. v. "seisin, n." "seisin, n.". *OED Online*. Oxford University Press.

6   *Baron and Feme: A Treatise of the Common Law. Concerning Husbands and Wives.* 2nd ed. (London, 1719), ECCO. Baron and feme are legal terms for husband and wife.

7   Under the power or governance of the husband.

8   "A writ of entry which lay for a woman against him to whom her husband aliened her lands or tenements in his lifetime. So called from the words of the writ– cui *ipsa* in vita *sua contradicere non potuit* &c.; (whom she, in his lifetime, could not gainsay, &c.)," Alexander M. Burrill, *A New Law Dictionary and Glossary* (New York: John S. Voorhies, 1850), 305. Google Books.

9   In most instances an "infant" was someone under the age of twenty one. See Blackstone, *Commentaries on the Laws of England*, Book 4, chapter 2, "Of the Persons Capable of Committing Crimes."

10   *The Treatise of Feme Coverts; or, The Lady's Law* (London, 1732): ECCO. The work was published in 1737 under the title *The Lady's Law, or The Treatise of Feme Coverts*.

Appendix Three

Excerpts from the Sarah Chapone–Samuel Richardson correspondence, with passages from *The Hardships of the English Laws in Relation to Wives*

There is no surviving evidence to suggest that Chapone disclosed to Samuel Richardson her publication of *The Hardships of the English Laws* fifteen years prior to the commencement of their correspondence. She admits to her authorship of *Remarks on Mrs. Muilman's Letter* in her first letter, expecting that he would recognize her handwriting. When he replies with his assurance that her secret is safe, he adds that he had inquired on reading *Remarks* if its author had published anything else, as it appeared to be "the Performance of one accustomed to write."[1] If this flattery elicited any further confidences, the letter has not survived. It is possible that the information might have been conveyed by her son John, or another of his correspondents from the Cotswold group. Whatever the case, in the lengthy discussions of women and the law in their correspondence of the early 1750s there is no reference to the work or her prior interest in and particular knowledge of the position of wives under England's common and civil law. Ironically, Richardson may well have known of *The Hardships of the English Laws in Relation to Wives* as he printed the *Weekly Miscellany* until early December 1736.[2]

The following parallel passages from Chapone's correspondence from the early 1750s, and the text of *The Hardships of the English Law in Relation to Wives*, contribute further evidence of her authorship.

1 From *The Hardships of the English Laws*

To divest a Man of all Property, and them exempt him from a Jail in Consequence of his Debts, is just such a Privilege in his Civil Capacity, as it would be in his Natural one, to divest him of all Pleasure, and in Return to decree that he should feel no Pain. As such Exemption from Pleasure and Pain would, in Effect, strike him out of *Being* as a *Man*, so such divesting him of all Property, with such Exemption from Payment of *Debts*, is, in Effect, to cut him off from being a Member of *Civil* Society (p. 43–44).

From Sarah Chapone to Samuel Richardson [undated, perhaps March–April, 1752]

"To deprive a Woman of her natural Liberty, under Pretence of keeping her out of Harms way, is just such a Favour as it would be, to derive a Man of all

Pleasure, and then, in return, graciously decree he should feel no Pain. As such Deprivation would strike a Man out of being, as a human Creature, who has the Image of God imprest upon him, so such Deprivation of Liberty would strike a Woman out of being, as a Member of Civil Society."[3]

2 From *The Hardships of the English Laws*

But if after all, these Representations should not be thought worthy the Consideration of the Legislature, or if they should be considered, and we should yet fail of obtaining any Relief; either because the Legislature cannot find proper Means, or wants the Inclination to give it; there is still one Part of my Sex, who may receive some Advantage from them; namely, the Unmarried, to whom I now Address myself, entreating them to consider the Hazards they run, when they venture an Alliance with the other Sex, who were designed by Nature for their *Counter-parts*, but who have taken upon themselves to be the *whole*, insomuch that they have voted us *Dead in Law*, except in criminal Causes. They do us indeed the Favour to consider us as real Persons, when they think fit to *burn* or *hang* us: This is *incorporating* with a Vengeance! *They swallowed us up quick, when they were so wrathfully displeased at us!*

But God be thanked, I have an Husband who lets me be *alive*, and gives me leave to be *some Body*, and to tell other People what I think they are.

I am persuaded there are many Wives in *England*, who by the Favour of their Husbands, are still in a State of *Existence*: And am also sensible, that some Wives have so little Apprehension of this Law of *Annihilation*, that they are in Fact the *freer* Agents of the two. But at Present I am not enquiring into Facts, I am reporting what I take to be the Law, in Order to have the Hardships of it known at least, that if they can't be amended, they may be avoided, by making Women more cautious, how they deliver themselves into the Hands of a Man, *lest he bring them to nothing.*

At the same Time that I warn my own Sex, I must do Justice to the other; and acknowledge, that I believe there are very many of them, to whom human Laws, as to their domestick Behaviour, are entirely superfluous (p. 47–48)

From Sarah Chapone (and John Chapone) to Samuel Richardson, September 21, 1754

[Chapone writes in the persona of her husband John Chapone, offering a rather tongue-in-cheek discussion of the powers of the husband, who is the wife's] . . . "summum jus.[4] Neither shall it be any bar to his being her summum jus, if it shall appear that he cannot be her summum bonum.[5] According to that establish'd rule that a wife is dead in law," [she continues in her own voice] "as wife, being nothing, I can know nothing; neither have I occasion to know anything; my conscience being provided with a supreme regulator, that is in cases where I may be allow'd to have a conscience; which, according to this sentence of annihilation pass'd upon wives, must be an extraordinary indulgence. "They swallow'd us up quick when they were so wrathfully displeas'd at us." This is incorporating with a vengeance! Effectually bringing us to nothing!

However, I am just now order'd to emerge into existence, and directed to present Mr. Chapone's best compliments—Love—and thanks to Mr. Richardson and his Lady."[6]

Notes

1 Samuel Richardson to Sarah Chapone, October 19, 1750. *Richardson Papers*, Reel 15. F48.E.6. Item 127.
2 Keith Maslen, *Samuel Richardson of London Printer: A Study of his Printing Based on Ornament Use and Business Accounts. Otago Studies in English* 7. Dunedin, NZ: University of Otago, 2001: 300.
3 *Richardson Papers*, Reel 15. F.48.E.6. Item 145.
4 A note is added at the bottom of the sheet, "Milton. Vid. Adam's speech to Eve God is thy Law, thou mine," a reference to *Paradise Lost* Book IV.
5 "Summum jus," the utmost rigour of the law, extreme severity; "summum bonum." the chief or supreme good. s.v. "summum jus, n." "summum bonum, n." *OED Online* Oxford University Press.
6 *Richardson Papers*, Reel 16. F.48.E.7. Item 13.

Bibliography

Archival Sources

Ballard Manuscripts. Vols. 41, 43. Bodleian Library, University of Oxford.

The Letters of Sarah Chapone. Gloucestershire Records Office, Gloucester, England.

Stanton with Snowshill Parish Records. Gloucestershire Public Record Office, Gloucester, England.

Wesley Family Papers, Methodist Archives, Manchester University Library.

Published Sources

Astell, Mary. "Some Reflections upon Marriage". In *Astell: Political Writings*. Edited by Patricia Springborg, 1–80. Cambridge: Cambridge University Press, 1996.

Atkyns, Robert. *The Ancient and Present State of Glostershire*. London, 1712. Eighteenth Century Collections Online. Gale Cengage.

Ayliffe, John. *A New Pandect of Roman Civil Law, as Anciently Established in that Empire*. London, 1734. Eighteenth Century Collections Online. Gale Cengage.

Backscheider, Paula. "Hanging on and Hanging in: Women's Struggle to Participate in Public Sphere Debate." In *Everyday Revolutions: Eighteenth-Century Women Transforming Public and Private*, edited by Diane E. Boyd and Marta Kvande, 30–66. Newark, DE: University of Delaware Press, 2008.

Bailey, Joanne. "Favoured or Oppressed? Married Women, Property and 'Coverture' in England, 1660–1800." *Continuity and Change* 17, no. 3 (2002): 351–372. doi: 10.1017/S0268416002004253.

Baker, J. H. "Why the History of English Law Has Not Been Finished." *Cambridge Law Journal* 59, no.1 (2000): 62–84. www.jstor.org/stable/4508643.

Barnard, Teresa. *Anna Seward: A Constructed Life: A Critical Biography*. Farnham, Surrey: Ashgate, 2009.

Baron and Feme: A Treatise of the Common Law. Concerning Husbands and Wives. 2nd ed. London, 1719. Eighteenth Century Collections Online. Gale Cengage.

Benson, Martin. *Bishop Benson's Survey of the Diocese of Gloucester, 1735–50*. Edited by John Findlay. The Bristol and Gloucestershire Archaeological Society, 2000.

Blackstone, William. *Commentaries on the Laws of England, A Facsimile of the First Edition of 1765–1769*. 4 Vols. Chicago, IL: University of Chicago Press, 1979.

The Book of Common Prayer, and Administration of the Sacraments, And Other Rites and Ceremonies of the Church, according to the use of the Church of England: together with the Psalter of David, Pointed as they are to be sung or said in Churches. London, 1731. Eighteenth Century Collections Online. Gale Cengage.

Brant, Clare. "Speaking of Women: Scandal and the Law in the Mid-Eighteenth Century." In *Women, Texts and Histories 1575–1760*, edited by Clare Brant and Diane Purkiss, 242–270. London: Routledge, 1992.

Breashears, Caroline. "Scandalous Categories: Classifying the Memoirs of Unconventional Women." *Philological Quarterly* 82, no. 2 (2003): 187–212.

Broad, Jacqueline. "'A Great Championess for Her Sex': Sarah Chapone on Liberty as Nondomination and Self-Mastery." *The Monist* 98, no. 1 (2015): 77–88. https://doi.org/10.1093/monist/onu009.

Burrill, Alexander M. *A New Law Dictionary and Glossary*. New York: John S. Voorhies, 1850. Google Books. https://books.google.ca/books?id=fo4zAQAAMAAJ&redir_esc=y.

Capp, Bernard. "Separate Domains? Women and Authority in Early Modern England." In *The Experience of Authority in Early Modern England*, edited by Paul Griffiths, Adam Fox, and Steve Hindle, 117–145. Basingstoke, UK: Macmillan, 1996.

Chapone, Hester [Mulso]. *The Posthumous Works of Mrs. Chapone. Containing her Correspondence with Mr. Richardson, A Series of Letters to Mrs. Elizabeth Carter, and Some Fugitive Pieces, Never Before Published.* Vol. 2. London: John Murray, 1807.

[Chapone, Sarah]. *The Hardships of the English Laws in Relation to Wives*. London, 1735.

——. *Remarks on Mrs. Muilman's Letter to the Right Honourable the Earl of Chesterfield. In a Letter to Mrs. Muilman.* By a Lady (London and Bath, 1750), Microform, "History of Women," New Haven, CT: Research Publications, 1975.

Clarke, Norma. "Elizabeth Elstob (1674–1752): England's First Professional Woman Historian?" *Gender & History* 17, no. 1 (2005): 210–220. doi: 10.1111/j.0953–5233.2005.00378.x.

——. *Queen of the Wits: A Life of Laetitia Pilkington*. London: Faber and Faber, 2008.

Clergy of the Church of England Database, s.v. "Robert Kirkham." http://theclergydatabase.org.uk/.

Coke, Edward. *The First Part of the Institutes of the Lawes of England; or, A Commentary upon Littleton*. London, 1628.

Cook, Daniel. "An Authoress to be Let." In *Women's Life Writing, 1700–1850: Gender, Genre and Authorship*, edited by Daniel Cook and Amy Culley, 39–54. Houndmills, UK: Palgrave Macmillan, 2012.

Crawford, Patricia and Laura Gowing, eds. *Women's Worlds in Seventeenth-Century England: A Sourcebook*. London: Routledge, 2000.

Crawford, Patricia and Sara Mendelson. *Women in Early Modern England*. Oxford: Clarendon, 1998.

Delany, Mary. *The Autobiography and Correspondence of Mary Granville, Mrs. Delany*. Edited by Lady Llanover. 3 Vols. London, 1861; 3 Vols. London, 1862.

Delany, Patrick. *The Present State of Learning, Religion, and Infidelity in Great-Britain*. Dublin, 1732. Eighteenth Century Collections Online. Gale Cengage.

——. *Revelation Examined with Candour*. Dublin, 1732. Eighteenth Century Collections Online. Gale Cengage.

De Montluzin, Emily Lorraine. *Attributions of Authorship in the* Gentleman's Magazine, *1731–1868: An Electronic Union List*. For Vol. 6 (1736). Charlottesville, Bibliographical Society of the University of Virginia, 2003. http://bsuva-epubs.org/bsuva/gm2/GMintro.html.

Dussinger, John. "Mary Astell's Revisions of *Some Reflections upon Marriage* (1730)." *The Papers of the Bibliographical Society of America* 107, no. 1 (2013): 49–79. www.jstor.org/stable/10.1086/680718.

Eaton, Barbara. *Yes, Papa! Mrs. Chapone and the Bluestocking Circle: A Biography of Hester Mulso-Mrs. Chapone (1727–1801), a Bluestocking.* London: Francis Boutle, 2012.

Eaves, T. C. Duncan and Ben D. Kimpel. *Samuel Richardson: A Biography.* Oxford: Clarendon, 1971.

E[dgar], T[homas]. *The Lawes Resolutions of Womens Rights.* London, 1632. Rpt. Amsterdam: Theatrum Orbis Terrarum; Norwood, NJ: Walter J. Johnson, 1979.

Erickson, Amy. *Women and Property in Early Modern England.* New York: Routledge, 1995.

The Gentleman's Magazine. February 1766, vol. 36.

Glover, Susan Paterson. "Further Reflections upon Marriage: Mary Astell and Sarah Chapone." In *Feminist Interpretations of Mary Astell*, edited by Alice Sowaal and Penny Weiss, 93–108. University Park, PA: Penn State University Press, 2016.

Great Britain. Court of Chancery. *Cases argued and adjudged in the High Court of Chancery. Published from the Manuscripts of Thomas Vernon, Late of the Middle Temple, Esq.* Dublin, 1726. Eighteenth Century Collections Online. Gale Cengage.

Green, V. H. H. *The Young Mr. Wesley: A Study of John Wesley and Oxford.* London: Edward Arnold, 1961.

Greenberg, Lynne A. *Legal Treatises. Essential Works for the Study of Early Modern Women. Series III, Part One.* Vol. 1, ix–lxiii. Farnham, UK: Ashgate, 2005.

Halifax, George Saville, Marquis of. *The Ladies New-year's Gift; or, Advice to a Daughter.* London, 1688.

Hannan, Leslie. "Collaborative Scholarship on the Margins: An Epistolary Network," *Women's Writing* 21, no. 3 (2014): 290–315. doi.org/10.1080/09699082.2014.925031.

Harris, Jocelyn. "Philosophy and Sexual Politics in Mary Astell and Samuel Richardson." *Intellectual History Review* 22, no. 3 (2012): 445–463. doi: 10.1080/17496977.2012. 695198.

Hayden, Ruth. *Mrs. Delany, Her Life and Her Flowers.* New York: New Amsterdam, 1992.

Joule, Victoria. "'Heroines of their own Romance': Creative Exchanges between Life-Writing and Fiction, the 'Scandalous Memoirists' and Charlotte Lennox." *Journal for Eighteenth-Century Studies* 37, no. 1 (2014): 37–52. doi: 10.1111/1754–0208.12033.

Keymer, Thomas. *Richardson's 'Clarissa' and the Eighteenth-Century Reader.* Cambridge: Cambridge University Press, 1992, 2004.

Laird, Mark and Alicia Weisberg-Roberts, eds. *Mrs. Delany & Her Circle.* New Haven, CT: Yale Center for British Art, Yale University Press, 2009.

Lea, Richard and Chris Miele with Gordon Higgott. *Danson House: The Anatomy of a Georgian Villa.* Swindon, UK: English Heritage, 2011.

Littleton, Thomas. *Tenures.* London, 1481/82.

Lyttelton, George. *Observations on the Conversion and Apostleship of St. Paul. In a letter to Gilbert West, Esq.* London, 1747.

Maslen, Keith. *An Early London Printing House at Work: Studies in the Bowyer Ledgers. With a Supplement to* The Bowyer Ornament Stock *(1973), an appendix on the Bowyer-Emonson Partnership, and 'Bowyer's Paper Stock Ledger', by Herbert Davis.* New York: The Bibliographical Society of America, 1993.

——. *Samuel Richardson of London Printer: A Study of his Printing Based on Ornament Use and Business Accounts. Otago Studies in English 7.* Dunedin, NZ: University of Otago, 2001.

Maslen, Keith and John Lancaster, eds. *The Bowyer Ledgers: The Printing Accounts of William Bowyer, Father and Son, reproduced on Microfiche: With a Checklist of*

Bowyer Printing, 1699–1777, a Commentary, Indexes, and Appendixes. London: The Bibliographical Society, 1991.

McDonnell, Michael. *The Registers of St. Paul's School 1509–1748*. London: Privately Printed for the Governors, 1977.

Montagu, Elizabeth. *Letters of Mrs. E. Montagu, with some of the Letters of her Correspondence*. Vol. 3. London: Cadell and Davies, 1813.

Muilman, Teresia Constantia [Phillips]. *An Apology for the Conduct of Mrs. Teresia Constantia Phillips, More Particularly that Part of it which relates to her Marriage with an Eminent Dutch Merchant*. 3 Vols. London, 1748–1749. Eighteenth Century Collections Online. Gale Cengage.

——. *A Letter humbly address'd to the Right Honourable the Earl of Chesterfield*. London, 1750. Eighteenth Century Collections Online. Gale Cengage.

Nussbaum, Felicity A. *The Autobiographical Subject: Gender and Ideology in Eighteenth-Century England*. Baltimore, MD: Johns Hopkins University Press, 1989.

Orlando: Women's Writing in the British Isles from the Beginnings to the Present. www.orlando.cambridge.org.

Orr, Clarissa Campbell. "The Sappho of Gloucestershire." In *Bluestockings Now! The Evolution of a Social Role*, edited by Deborah Heller, 91–110. Farnham, UK: Ashgate, 2015.

Pegge, Samuel. *An Historical Account of that Venerable Monument of Antiquity the Textus Roffensis; including Memoirs of the Learned Saxonists Mr. William Elstob and his Sister.* London, 1784. Eighteenth Century Collections Online. Gale Cengage.

Perry, Ruth. *The Celebrated Mary Astell: An Early English Feminist*. Chicago, IL: University of Chicago Press, 1986.

——. Introduction to *Memoirs of Several Ladies of Great Britain who have been Celebrated for their Writings or Skill in the Learned Languages, Arts and Science*, by George Ballard. 12–48. Detroit, MI: Wayne State University Press, 1985.

——. "Review of *Women Writers and the Early Modern British Political Tradition*, ed. Hilda Smith." *American Historical Review* 105, no. 1 (2000): 276–278. doi: 10.2307/2652568.

Pilkington, Laetitia. *Memoirs of Laetitia Pilkington*. 2 Vols. Edited by A. C. Elias, Jr. Athens, GA: University of Georgia Press, 1997.

Probert, Rebecca. *Marriage Law and Practice in the Long Eighteenth Century: A Reassessment*. Cambridge: Cambridge University Press, 2009.

Rack, Henry D. *Reasonable Enthusiast: John Wesley and the Rise of Methodism*. 3rd ed. London: Epworth Press, 2002.

Richards, Jennifer and Alison Thorne. Introduction to *Rhetoric, Women and Politics in Early Modern England*, 1–24. London: Routledge, 2007.

Richardson, Samuel. *Papers of Samual* [sic] *Richardson*. The Forster and Dyce Collections. Part Two: 18th Century Manuscripts. Reels 15 and 16. Harvester Press Microform Publications, 1986.

——. *Selected Letters of Samuel Richardson*. Edited by John Carroll. Oxford: Clarendon, 1964.

The Right of British Subjects, to Petition and Apply to their Representatives, Asserted and Vindicated. In a Letter to *****. London, 1733. Eighteenth Century Collections Online. Gale Cengage.

Rowe, Elizabeth. *Devout Exercises of the Heart: In Meditation and Soliloquy, Prayer and Praise*. London, 1737. Eighteenth Century Collections Online. Gale Cengage.

Rudolph, Julia. *Common Law and Enlightenment in England, 1689–1750*. Woodbridge, UK: Boydell Press, 2013.

Schellenberg, Betty. *Literary Coteries and the Making of Modern Print Culture 1740–1790*. Cambridge: Cambridge University Press, 2016.

Sherlock, Thomas. *The Use and Intent of Prophecy, in the Several Ages of the World*. London, 1732. Eighteenth Century Collections Online. Gale Cengage.

A Short Apology For the Common Law; Together with Proposals for Removing the Expence and Delay of Equity Proceedings. London, 1731. Eighteenth Century Collections Online. Gale Cengage.

Shrifin, Susan, ed. *"The Wandering Life I Led": Essays on Hortense Mancini, Duchess Mazarin and Early Modern Women's Border Crossings*. Newcastle upon Tyne, UK: Cambridge Scholars Publishing, 2009.

Simpson, A. W. B. *A History of the Common Law of Contract: The Rise and Fall of the Action of Assumpsit*. Oxford: Clarendon Press, 1987.

Smollett, Tobias. *The Adventures of Peregrine Pickle. In which are included, Memoirs of a Lady of Quality*. 3 Vols. London, 1751.

The Spectator. Edited by Donald F. Bond. Vol. 2. Oxford: Clarendon, 1965.

Stackhouse, Thomas. *The Miseries and Great Hardships of the Inferior Clergy, in and about London. And a modest plea for the rights, and better usage; in a Letter to the Right Reverend Father in God, John Lord Bishop of London*. London, 1722. Eighteenth Century Collections Online. Gale Cengage.

Staves, Susan. "Church of England Clergy and Women Writers." *Huntington Library Quarterly* 65, no. 1/2 (2002): 81–103. www.jstor.org.myaccess.library.utoronto.ca/stable/3817732.

——. "'The Liberty of a She-Subject of England': Rights Rhetoric and the Female Thucydides." *Cardozo Studies in Law and Literature* 1, no. 2 (1989): 161–183. doi: 10.1080/1535685X.1989.11015651.

——. *Married Women's Separate Property in England, 1660–1833*. Cambridge, MA: Harvard University Press, 1990.

Stone, Lawrence. *Uncertain Unions: Marriage in England, 1660–1753*. Oxford: Oxford University Press, 1992.

Stretton, Tim. "Coverture and Unity of Person in Blackstone's *Commentaries*." In *Blackstone and his Commentaries: Biography, Law, History*, edited by Wilfrid Prest, 111–127. Oxford: Hart, 2009.

Stretton, Tim and Krista J. Kesselring, eds. *Married Women and the Law: Coverture in England and the Common Law World*. Montreal: McGill-Queen's Press, 2013.

Thomason, Laura E. *The Matrimonial Trap: Eighteenth-Century Women Writers Redefine Marriage*. Lewisburg: Bucknell University Press, 2014.

Thompson, Lynda M. *The "Scandalous Memoirists": Constantia Phillips, Laetitia Pilkington and the Shame of "Publick Fame."* Manchester, UK: Manchester University Press, 2000.

"A Tract on the Unreasonableness of the Law in Regard to Wives." *The Columbian Magazine*, January pp. 22–27, February pp. 61–65, March pp. 126–129, April pp. 186–189, May pp. 243–246, 1788. https://archive.org/details/columbianmagazin21788phil.

A Treatise of Feme Coverts; or, The Lady's Law. London, 1732. Eighteenth Century Collections Online. Gale Cengage.

"Utopiensis, Bernardus." *A Second Dissertation on the Liberty of Preaching Granted to Women by the People called Quakers*. Dublin, 1739. Eighteenth Century Collections Online. Gale Cengage.

The Weekly Miscellany, 1736, 1737. London, England. *17th and 18th Century Burney Collection Newspapers*. Gale Cengage.

Wesley, John. *A Sermon preached at St. Mary's in Oxford, On Sunday, September 21, 1735*. London, 1735.

——. *The Works of John Wesley*. Vol. 20. Journal and Diaries III (1743–1754). Edited by W. Reginald Ward and Richard P. Heitzenrater. Nashville, TN: Abingdon Press, 1991.

Wesley, Samuel. *Dissertationes in Librum Jobi*. London, 1736.

Wesley, Susanna. *Susanna Wesley: The Complete Writings*. Edited by Charles Wallace, Jr. New York: Oxford University Press, 1997.

Wheatly, Charles. *A Rational Illustration of the Book of Common Prayer of the Church of England*. 5th ed. London, 1728. Eighteenth Century Collections Online. Gale Cengage.

Wollaston, William. *The Religion of Nature Delineated*. London, 1722. Eighteenth Century Collections Online. Gale Cengage.

Wood, Thomas. *A New Institute of the Imperial or Civil Law*. 4th ed. London, 1730. Eighteenth Century Collections Online. Gale Cengage.

Wright, Nancy E., Margaret W. Ferguson, and A. R. Buck, eds. *Women, Property, and the Letters of the Law in Early Modern England*. Toronto: University of Toronto Press, 2004.

Index

n refers to chapter end note, fn refers to footnote.

Printed in Great Britain
by Amazon

38920839R00079